W9-BFO-102

What Patients Taught Me

What Patients Taught Me

A Medical Student's Journey

AUDREY YOUNG, MD

SASQUATCH BOOKS
SEATTLE

Printed in Canada
Published by Sasquatch Books
Distributed by Publishers Group West
12 11 10 09 08 07 06 05 04   6 5 4 3 2 1

Book design: Stewart A. Williams

Library of Congress Cataloging-in-Publication Data
Young, Audrey, M.D.
          What patients taught me : a medical student's journey / by Audrey
Young.
          p. cm.
          ISBN 1-57061-396-6
          1. Young, Audrey, M.D. 2. Medical students—United States—
Biography. 3. Medicine, Rural. 4. Physician and patient. I. Title.

R729.5.R87Y68 2004
610'.92—dc22
[B]
                                                                    2004048249

Sasquatch Books ~ 119 South Main Street, Suite 400
Seattle, WA 98104 ~ (206) 467-4300
www.sasquatchbooks.com ~ custserv@sasquatchbooks.com

For my parents, Peter and Sioeling Young

Contents

When you bring first-year medical students to the wards, you tell them the patient is at the center and they look at you like you're crazy. They cannot conceive of how the patient could not be at the center. The patient is the reason they've chosen medicine. I want to tell them, wait until third year.

ERIKA GOLDSTEIN, MD
ASSOCIATE PROFESSOR OF MEDICINE
CHAIR, INTRODUCTION TO CLINICAL MEDICINE
UNIVERSITY OF WASHINGTON

Preface

These are true stories. The identities of actual patients and doctors have been slightly altered. Stories like these happen every day in remote places and less often in the hospitals that produce tomorrow's physicians.

Thirty years ago the University of Washington bravely began sending medical students to work alongside small-town general physicians in hopes of reversing the steep drop in rural doctors. The experiment raised eyebrows across the academic establishment. Prominent teaching physicians predicted the medical school would turn out sub-par graduates, but the rogue university pressed ahead.

By the time I enrolled at the University of Washington in the mid-1990s, more than one hundred physician groups in the remote Pacific Northwest were teaching medical students. I received most of my clinical training in these rural places. The work was physically taxing and the depth of human suffering often intense. My experiences were never impersonal, though, as is commonly the charge in medical training these days.

At first I wrote about patients to process days filled with sick and dying people. At night in the student apartment I sat at my boxy old Macintosh computer with a five-inch screen and tried to come to terms with a child with cancer, a grandmother with eroding memory.

Later in medical school, I volunteered at a hospital in •

southern Africa and emailed group letters back to the United States about the impossible conditions there. A friend and fellow medical student who had worked with me in rural Montana emailed me back, "Keep writing. This could become something." Here was my spark.

I wrote and rewrote. Finally I recognized that the only thing to really make doctoring a human act is time spent with patients. Patients teach things that the wisest and most revered physicians cannot, and their lessons are in this book.

CHAPTER 1

Bethel

———————

The first call crackled across the emergency scanner at midnight.

"This is Aniak," a voice reported. "I have a twenty-one-year-old male, seven minutes status post gunshot wound to the left ear. Unconscious. Pupils 2 mm on the left, 3 mm on the right. Blood pressure is 178 over 100."

"How is he breathing?" the attending doctor asked, her eyes fixed to the floor.

"Breathing thirty a minute, oxygen sat is 100 percent on a 6 liter mask."

"Is he moving anything? Legs? Fingers?" The doctor raised an impatient eyebrow.

She looked expectantly at the scanner, a silver metal grate on the wall. She was tall, wire-thin, and she wore hiking boots. We were standing in the emergency department's small triage room, a stale space with shelves of textbooks worn at the spines.

"No, not responding at all," the health aide said. "I have IV fluids going and gave a dose of ceftriaxone."

A moment later he added, "Awaiting medivac."

"We're working on it," she said. "Your patient needs to get here *now*."

The attending doctor exhaled audibly, then picked up the telephone and asked for the medivac pilot. I shifted nervously in the hot room as I imagined the health aide eating with his family when the loud cracking gunshot sounded through the village. The aide stood automatically and noise drained from the room. He went out the door and up a gravelly hill. In the clinic, he switched on the waiting room lights. The hallway leading to examination rooms in back was dark and faintly blue in the night.

Moments later a low-riding pickup truck stopped at the clinic door with a young Eskimo man lying in the back. The driver vaulted out of the cab. Together, aide and driver carried the man into the waiting room and arranged him on a gurney on the floor. The patient had been drinking with his cousins when he walked away for a moment, laughing, and shot himself in the left ear with a .22-caliber handgun. Now clots of dark blood stuck in his hair and quick breaths popped from his mouth. His right eyebrow was split open where the bullet exited.

The health aide came on the scanner again.

"Ready for transport. Awaiting medivac," he repeated urgently.

A pilot wearing a blue jumpsuit came in the triage room. The pilot's face was shadowy with stubble, his movements quick and automatic like the medics and doctors.

"What do you think?" the attending doctor said.

"We can't," the pilot said.

"The patient's rapidly going downhill," the attending protested. "He's got to get here or to Anchorage."

"It's not safe," the pilot said. They swapped tense glances, then he walked to the scanner and pushed the red TALK button.

"Aniak, this is medivac. We can't land in this weather. The cloud ceiling is too low."

The report came back rushed and desperate from the village one hundred miles upriver: "Pupils 2 mm on the left, 4 mm on the right. Blood pressure 180 over 100. Heart rate 54."

The attending stepped in quickly and said, "What fluids are you running?"

"Lactated Ringer's wide open, about a third of the bag in."

"Slow that down to about 100 cc per hour."

"Okay, copy."

The pilot turned to the attending and said, "National Guard won't fly either."

"Someone has to get him or he's going to die," she said.

The pilot tilted his head to the side for a moment, holding her gaze. "Someone could die just trying to land the airplane," he said. After a moment he added, "I'll make some calls."

When he checked back twenty minutes later, the attending and I were in the operating room with a boy who'd split his lip open straight down to tooth. The pilot reported that one by one, local private carriers had refused the flight to Aniak.

Now the health aide was patched through to the operating room.

"This is Aniak," he said somberly. "Right pupil is 5 mm. Anchorage will land at 3:30." The National Weather Service had advised that clouds would blow over as morning came on. A private company had finally agreed to fly, the aide said. He would accompany the patient to the regional hospital in Anchorage.

The attending continued to pull blue nylon thread through

the boy's velvety skin. The radio fell silent and I understood that a turning point had come and gone. The clock on the wall behind the operating table flashed 1:00 a.m. and suddenly I felt the inevitability that goes with endings of bad dreams. I thought desperately of sleepy villagers climbing into their trucks and turning engines over. They pointed vehicles along the runway to illuminate the landing site and guide the rescue aircraft. With motors idling, heat blasting, and wives sitting solemnly in the passenger seats, they huddled in thick jackets hoping to save the dying young man.

I thought about the airplane lifting off into the dull, dark sky and the unconscious man wrapped in bloody blankets under the ambulance's fluorescent lights, a mother and father and a village of brothers waiting in an endless night.

In years of remembering, the most realistic part of the story became the scene that took place in Anchorage, hundreds of miles away. The nurses began the resuscitation when the patient's heart rate faded away to almost nothing. Someone pumped at his chest, trying to restart the sluggish organ. Doctors sprinted down the hospital hallways and an anesthesiologist positioned himself at the patient's head, squeezing a loud rubber bag that forced fresh air into the patient's lungs. The floor became slippery with saline, plastic wrappers, and syringes. His heart would not restart even after three forceful electric shocks burnt through the skin of his chest and caused him to levitate momentarily. Finally he died with a clump of people bent over his failed body. He was left alone, a sheet thrown hastily over him, waiting for the mortician to take him on a stretcher. Afterward, the nurses and doctors talked of what had been done during the resuscitation, about whether the atropine and compressions had been too much or too little. They did not talk about the family, due to arrive on the first plane in the morning.

Sometimes they never even learned the patient's name.

In the University of Washington brochure for prospective medical students that I received during my last year of college, there was a full-page, black-and-white photograph of a jeep heading down a long rural road. Stands of cedar press up along both sides of the jeep and the windshield is murky with dust except where a wiper blade has cleared a terse arc. The sun shines so brightly that the pavement looks white, and the mood is one of determination. The image perfectly articulated my vision of doctoring. I tore out the photograph, pinned it to the wall above my mattress, and gazed at it often while waiting to hear whether the medical school would interview me for the first-year class.

The picture represented nothing outwardly about me or my hopes for medicine. I had first imagined becoming a doctor in the foggy swirl of high school in suburban Seattle, where my peers were the children of lawyers and physicians. I heard tales about a classmate's neurologist father and became intrigued with the brain and people who suffered aberrant brain function. The world of patients, doctors, and disease was otherwise mysterious to me. I knew nobody personally who practiced medicine and thought of hospitals as places where people emerged with scars and bandages. My family's line of work was computers, and dinner conversation at our house was typically about problems of coding and computer language.

Nevertheless, I set off for college at Berkeley feeling intellectual resonance for medicine. Berkeley was a place where many students entertained at least evanescent thoughts of becoming a doctor. Among the most popular premedical courses was a medical ethics lecture that drew four hundred students every semester, and the science classes I enrolled into were highly competitive. With each passing semester, the number of pre-med students was roughly halved, owing to a grade curve where C is truly middle of the pack, and soon my chances of gaining admission to medical school were in serious jeopardy. After two or three freshman flameouts and a summer of soul-searching, I turned myself over to organic chemistry and physics and scraped by with marks that would not disqualify me altogether.

At Berkeley, a certain world materialized around me. Homelessness and poverty lived in plain view along the streets to campus. I heard stories of families, cultures, and hardships from students in my dormitory, parents in local schools, and people on the street. I sat in history seminars and volunteered in inner-city schools and clinics to discover the place where I lived and what I wished to contribute. I read newspapers and talked with everyone I could about socioeconomic inequality, which I'd never really experienced before, and which had come to trouble me deeply. I began to conceive of how medicine might be a tool toward equality. Later I organized a class on health care and poverty and felt I'd finally hit the mark: I wanted to be an urban doctor for neglected populations. When the University of Washington offered me an interview, I flew home to Seattle full of my heady ideas.

I arrived twenty minutes early on the appointed day and eagerly gave my name at the medical school dean's office. The receptionist looked disinterestedly at me and pointed to the waiting area, and my hands turned cold. Six candidates would interview for medical school that afternoon and the two already idling in lounge chairs wore sharp, dark suits and looked ready to ace the interview. I sat with the suits and became enfolded into their conversation. The buzz on the interview trail that year was about a Cleveland medical school that had done away with the two-year detour through lecture hall, followed by two years of intensive patient care, as was standard in medical education everywhere else. The new Cleveland curriculum entangled classroom learning with the hospital wards in all four years of medical school, with the idea of keeping students focused on the patient. Just then I wished I'd considered other schools and hadn't arrived back home in Seattle so fresh and untested. Such was my naivete that I had not considered how I would learn to care for patients or exactly which skills and attributes would make me into a good doctor. Now the conversation turned to the day's task.

One of the suits crossed his legs and leaned back and said, "I hear this is the hardest interview."

"I hear they get you with ethics questions," the other said. "And managed care."

I had heard the same. From one candidate who'd taken a beating, I learned of a potential question about withdrawing care on a brain-dead patient, and from a friend I heard of a question about abortion. I'd mulled over possible responses to these queries and guessed what similar lines of questioning might arise. But I hadn't prepared with a practice interview or actually organized my talking points on these tender issues, where an ill-rendered opinion could throw my chances.

I was nodding in agreement when the receptionist called my name. I jumped to my feet. Both suits froze momentarily, then looked up and wished me luck. I followed the receptionist down a corridor into an institutional-style room where three men from the admissions committee waited.

A copy of my file sat in front of each doctor with my personal statement on top. In the long room we commenced a round of handshaking. The senior physician, a tenured professor of medicine, made a few jerky motions of offering coffee, and then we all sat simultaneously. The youngest member of the panel had a tanned face and graying hair and I watched him glance down at my personal statement. A sigh rose in my throat. I had written the statement in the tone of a manifesto, describing how I would use medicine to redress social inequalities in urban neighborhoods. Then the young physician launched his barrage. How did I propose to pay the costs of fixing social inequalities, he wondered. Did I think violence was a medical problem? What were solutions for social disasters like children without parents and teenagers doing jail time? I gave the best answers I could, answers that on later review felt highly imperfect. A feline expression settled upon the quiet member of the panel, who managed a hint of a smile through the entire interview and piped in with the occasional encouraging question. The senior professor of medicine fell asleep until just before the interview concluded, when he ruffled his feathers, opened his eyes, and pointed out what my answers lacked.

The interview ended after an hour and a half and I heard nothing from the committee for months. In the meantime I considered the Peace Corps or a history Ph.D. I was offered a job teaching American history at an inner-city high school in Houston. Then, as the curtain fell on my college days at Berkeley, a letter from the medical school appeared on the kitchen counter. I cringed and prepared for disappointing news as I reached for the slim business-sized envelope that held, by feel, a single sheet of paper. I circled the apartment holding the envelope and debated whether to throw it into the recycling bin directly or to look at it first. Finally I opened the letter and intuited with a squint that I hadn't been rejected outright. In another moment, I read that I'd been ranked second on the waiting list. My hands began to shake. I did not know what the waiting list meant, but I was suddenly optimistic about my chances of gaining admission to medical school.

Another business-sized envelope arrived a week later, this one joyfully hefty, and I understood the significance immediately. My reply went out the next morning.

A month later, a letter arrived from Seattle soliciting twenty volunteers to spend first year in Pullman, Washington, a farm town situated on the Idaho border. For those wishing to get farther afield, the Bozeman, Montana, site could accommodate two additional students. The away classrooms were smaller, with more individual attention for every student, the letter said. The dispersed arrangement was part of the WWAMI system, a program to train medical students from the Pacific Northwest to practice as rural doctors. I rejected outright the idea of spending an entire year in a rural town and wrote back my strong preference for being in Seattle, having no idea the real competition was for the rural slots. In due time the school granted me the Seattle assignment and I forgot about the matter.

First year commenced in a rush and I turned faintly manic to stay afloat of seven crash courses on human biology. I spent my days sitting in a hard plastic chair high in the audience at the first-year student lecture hall, a latte cooling next to me, my notebook filling with fresh notes. I perpetually fell behind on reading, fretted over everything slipping past, and forever crammed for exams. My world became the labyrinth of classrooms and laboratories in the medical center's T-wing, the cold fresh air of the bike ride home, a drawbridge by the hospital ringing and clanging as it admitted a sailboat through the Montlake Cut. I settled into the idea that doctoring meant fixing bodies with science.

A cadaver became my first patient. My classmates and I spent long hours dissecting the body in whatever fashion served to teach human anatomy. We sawed through the sternum and squeezed gloved hands around blood vessels traveling to and from the heart. We eviscerated the upper digestive tract to examine the colon more carefully. Our professors concealed each cadaver's hands and face behind tightly wound bandage wrap, and the remnant body seemed more husk than human.

As the year progressed, we moved on to living bodies. I first practiced the physical examination on classmate friends who were running partners and soccer teammates, and I learned to divine sounds of the human heart, the rustle of lungs, watery noises of intestines. Later the school hired trained actors to test our skills. Like many first-year students, though, I had not interacted with real patients in a clinic or hospital setting and after a bookish year of physiology and pharmacology, I still considered myself an observer in that world of doctors and disease.

The first glimpses of the clinical world came slowly. I signed on to shadow a family physician in a working-class immigrant neighborhood and volunteered in a student-run free clinic. The prospect of rural medicine surfaced anew with the offering of an intensive small-town experience during the summer after first year. I began to hear more about wwami, a system of clinics, doctors, and classrooms across the Pacific Northwest that exposed students to remote medicine, and later I learned that entire counties in Alaska and Montana lacked even a single doctor.

For once I tried to imagine myself within the wwami landscape of Washington, Wyoming, Alaska, Montana, and Idaho. I had to consult a map to remember where Wyoming is, and I didn't like the racially divisive things I'd read in newspapers about Idaho. The idea of wwami-land still clashed with my idea of doctoring. When I studied the maps a little longer, though, I was surprised to discover that wwami-land enveloped more than one-quarter of the U.S. landmass. Seattle, home to many of the region's doctors, was just one speck in a corner of the Pacific Northwest. Maybe the imbalance between rural

and urban physicians was more significant than I had realized. Maybe there were similarities between inner-city urban
medicine and medicine in a remote place.

So I tossed my name into a lottery for summer placement
and held my breath. A couple months later WWAMI dangled
its offer of an expenses-paid month at a remote Eskimo out-
post in the Alaska bush. I hadn't entirely gotten over my discomfort with small towns, but really, how could I say no?

After classes finished in June, I boarded a series of airplanes
for a tiny town called Bethel, on Alaska's Bering Sea coast. On
the ground in Bethel, brown tundra rolled out in every direction, and rooted to that vast space was a Yupik Eskimo civilization in upheaval. Bethel, the Yupik hub, had a population
of four thousand and was closer to Siberia across the Bering
Strait than to the state capital, Juneau. Bethel had seven miles
of paved roads; the pavement became sandy muck beyond the
high school. The only means of long-distance transportation
in summer was the small airplane. In winter, airplanes were
often grounded by subzero temperatures, but Yupiks travelled
long distances overland by dogsled and snowmachine.

Suddenly I was thousands of miles from the world I understood. I was a twenty-three-year-old kid with little life experience. I fretted over the smell and feel of disease and was
nervous about placing my hands on human bodies. But I was
equally eager to begin caring for patients. I looked forward to
speaking the language of medicine and trying to make basic
treatment decisions. Above all I hoped to experience human
drama and emotion as it unfolded. These were the real-life
anchors of medicine to my mind.

The first morning, I reported to the Bethel Family Practice Clinic dressed in jeans, hiking boots, a flannel shirt, and a stethoscope, the standard garb for doctors working on the tundra. My brain was full of facts about malaria and Rocky Mountain Spotted Fever and motor reflex pathways, and I fumbled to organize a human being's story and interpret x-rays and blood tests. Some afternoons and evenings I rode my single-speed bicycle to the native hospital a mile up the damp sandy road. At all hours the hospital bustled with Yupik Eskimo patients arriving from tiny villages battened down onto plateaus and hillsides across the Yukon-Kuskokwim Delta, a parcel of western Alaska equal in size, at forty thousand square miles, to the state of Virginia. Often the patients had flown in from a hundred miles away and suffered serious illnesses that hadn't responded to the health aide's measures or the village shaman's hands, diseases that hadn't melted back with time.

Now I began meeting people I never could have imagined and became privy to the severe conditions of their lives, the depths of illness they carried about from day to day. I would put my hands to the ground under their feet and smell the fresh earth, cross the tundra in tiny airplanes that moved like leaves on the wind, and mingle with others in the streets of Yupik villages.

I was becoming a doctor.

The first lessons came from watching and listening. While I idled on the obstetrics ward one morning waiting for a new mother to change into a hospital gown, a senior obstetrics nurse chatted about her eight years at the native hospital.

Like many of the hospital's medical and nursing staff, she'd come to Bethel after putting in time in the Lower 48. She had cared for a thousand pregnant women and delivered their kids, so she knew labor and delivery in a deeply intuitive way. Despite that, she still had trouble interpreting Yupik faces. Laboring Yupik mothers walked the hospital ward noise-lessly, stopping when a contraction came on and taking short audible breaths. When she escorted mothers into the birthing suite and checked the progress of labor, she frequently found the baby crowning, its scalp visible in the birth canal, half an hour from being born. She said that Yupik mothers' expres-sions remained remote through contractions, the frequent examinations, and even delivery.

"But they're grateful when you offer pain medication," she said, her face firm and glinting.

The nurse had tailored her comments specifically to the patient I waited to meet, a twenty-six-year-old mother named Elena Carie who had delivered one week before. Elena's labor had proceeded uneventfully and the child had weathered her contractions and the acrobatics of birth with aplomb. Dur-ing the delivery, the baby's shoulder tore the back of Elena's vagina, and the obstetrician had stitched up the fragmented pieces. Elena went home the next afternoon with the thriving newborn.

She returned now because urinating caused her such severe, lancinating pain that she hadn't relieved herself in twenty-four hours, the nurse said.

I walked into the examination suite with Dr. Hannah, the attending doctor with a closely trimmed red beard, who had hustled over to the ward from the emergency department. He was in the midst of a twelve-hour shift that was as predictably busy as ever and filled with critically sick patients. Dr. Hannah had come to Bethel after his residency in Atlanta was finished a year ago, and he planned to stay through the following spring. Like most of the attending physicians at Bethel, he was a family practitioner, one of the hardy young doctors who'd picked Bethel for the wildly different setting, the breadth of practice, and the energetic colleagues. I hadn't worked with him yet but had seen him riding his bike to and from the hospital under clear skies and in pounding rain and I was taken by this spare determination.

In the examination room, Elena sat on the table with her legs held tightly together underneath a light-blue paper sheet. I felt my eyes magnetically pulled to the sheet and then I forced myself to gaze up to her oddly emotionless face. Her parents stood at the head of the bed.

"I understand you're having pain," Dr. Hannah said. "When did this start?"

Elena registered the question and drew her mouth to a point. She did not speak for several moments and then her mother sighed and said, "Since the baby was born. But it is getting much worse, especially today."

"Any fever?"

"She has been hot," the mother said. The doctor looked at the floor.

"Your appetite?"

"Nothing," the mother said.

"Elena, can you tell me, do you have discharge from the

vagina?" he asked. The look on his face sharpened.

Elena was staring at the ceiling now and she shifted uneasily under the paper sheet.

"Nothing," her mother answered, drawing the word out in a husky breath. A quiver passed over Dr. Hannah's brow.

Dr. Hannah switched on the bright overhead lamp and pulled the sheet back over Elena's legs, which she held together defiantly. With a gloved hand, he firmly touched the inside of one thigh. Tears flashed in Elena's eyes and I cringed inwardly as she allowed him to push her legs apart. A thick yellow-brown liquid had leaked from her and puddled on the table. Dr. Hannah placed a metal speculum to examine the inside of her vagina and showed me that the tissue torn during birth had turned a metallic gray, with very little healthy pink color remaining. Stitches had melted through the dying tissue and lay thoughtlessly and randomly like bits of litter, little loops of blue thread scattered between the tissue layers. Dr. Hannah clicked the speculum open to reveal the cervix and a sharp sulfuric smell issued forth.

Dr. Hannah glanced at me, then back at Elena. He looked like he had another question for her but he shook his head instead, gently removed the speculum, felt her uterus with his hands, then replaced the blue sheet over her lower body. He twisted around to locate the nurse and ordered that Elena receive doses of penicillin, gentamicin, and clindamycin, three intravenous antibiotics, immediately. He turned back to the patient and explained that she would need urgent surgery to clean out the infection, which had spread deeply in the birth canal.

Elena wiped her eyes with the back of her hand. Her mother's cheeks suddenly flushed and she turned to Dr. Hannah.

"Who will do the surgery?" she asked.

"We'll ask the doctor who delivered the baby," Dr. Hannah said.

"Not him," the mother said. "He made a mistake."

"Alright," Dr. Hannah said. He moved toward the sink. "We'll find somebody." Then we went out of the suite and to the front of the ward, to where nurses wrote their charts. Before we sat, he paged a family doctor who performed basic obstetrical surgery.

"Can you believe this?" Dr. Hannah said. "This is not unusual here." He told me that at the vast county hospital where he trained, he rarely saw patients with illnesses as advanced as those in Bethel.

The consulting surgeon was a small, fit, soft-spoken man in his late forties who wore a flannel shirt open at the collar. He had walked over from the clinic to discuss the case. Dr. Hannah rapidly began to report on Elena's condition, running sentences together and taking little gasps of breaths. He chose vivid descriptors: her difficulty urinating, the 103 degree F fever, metal gray vaginal tissue, copious pus, unbearable pain at the lightest touch.

The surgeon murmured as Dr. Hannah gave his assessment: "She's got hemodynamically stable sepsis from endometritis and regional soft tissue infection. She's getting pen, clinda, and gent, and fluids."

The surgeon frowned and said, "She needs debridement."

"Oh yes."

"I'll see her and arrange for operating room staff in the next hour or two."

"Thanks very much."

The surgeon stood briskly and nodded again. "It's a wonder all women don't get post-partum infections," he said sympathetically, and moved toward Elena's room.

The short interaction affected me greatly. Dr. Hannah had condensed our complicated twenty-minute visit with patient and family into a very brief story of illness and evaluation of Elena's condition. The code of words and facts that passed between the two men had convinced the consulting doctor to put everything on hold, including an entire morning's clinic patients, to undertake a complicated surgery that would heal Elena in a week and protect her childbearing abilities.

I had just seen a story motivate a physician and make things happen, and now I understood that doctors must be good storytellers. The doctor doesn't attempt the craft and cunning of a writer, who hooks and captivates through turns of plot and beautiful language. The doctor wants to tell a story that gives away the ending in the first few sentences and then instructs succinctly on specifics of the individual and his or her disease. Obtaining the story could be challenging with reticent patients and dominating family members, and I appreciated that Dr. Hannah needed tact and skill to flesh out Elena's story.

Learning to tell that story seemed another matter altogether. During first year, I practiced taking the social history of hospitalized patients and the conversations centered on home, family, and occupation. The conversations often led to tales of conflict and repair, which I wrote out as a dry accounting of a patient's life. Later in the year, we were coached to interview the patient on his or her acute illness and then instructed to integrate the medical and social angles. The basic idea was to establish a human context for illness, which made good sense to me. But the Yupik story was wrapped in a murky context, and what I could make out was a story very much about the place.

In the chilly charter airplane I sat next to a Yupik health aide named Anna Phillip, a thirty-four-year old single working mother who was born and raised in a tundra village and now lived in Bethel. An elderly Yupik couple huddled on the seat behind us and sacks of village mail were piled behind them. The old woman made fast, furtive glances out the window. Anna's boyfriend, Roland, sat quietly in front. The pilot closed the passenger door with a hard shove and walked around the plane, fit himself into his seat, and turned the ignition. The small Cessna bounced softly as the propellers began to churn. The old woman gasped and whispered something in Yupik, and Anna turned smiling to me and said sympathetically, "She's scared of flying." I shivered in my ski parka, which I had worn on Anna's advice. Despite it being summer and the sun still high in the Alaska sky, I could see my breath in the cold air. We were flying to Anna's birth village of St. Mary's, situated about one hundred miles north of Bethel along the Yukon River, to spend the weekend with her family. For the occasion, Anna had changed into an Eskimo dress done in floral fabric that fell just above the knee, a style that Yupiks called kuspuk, and she wore black leggings underneath the dress.

Anna had told me that St. Mary's was a typical Yupik village, with a population of four hundred. She had one brother, who lived in the village with his wife. She had grown up in St. Mary's and then gone to high school in Bethel, boarding in the city as all Eskimo children were required to do at that time. She had trained as a health aide at the Bethel junior college, and except for two years when she had been briefly married to a white man and lived in Seward, she had lived her adult life in Bethel. Now she was the health aide at the busy family practice clinic. Her jobs varied from drawing blood to translating to serving as health educator, and she patiently taught me skills like taking blood pressures and injecting vaccines. At times she was the only link between the attending doctor, a native Californian, and patients who spoke Yupik exclusively. She was unmistakably Yupik herself, with a petite physique and a bowlegged gait that turned sturdy and sure on the unsteady tundra. Her short, black hair fell in wisps from the crown of her head, and her eyes became squinty and bright when she smiled. She spoke English with a distinct Yupik accent, drawing out the last syllable of a word and letting the final sound fade away to nothing, her English rising and falling with a musical cadence.

Now the pilot maneuvered out of the parking space and turned right onto the runway. The plane hummed loudly as we accelerated. I felt the plane catch and lift in the wind and we ascended over Bethel. From the air I traced the airport road to the back neighborhoods and glimpsed the trailer house where I stayed and the pickup truck parked out front. Then the houses grew small and everything below turned into straw-colored tundra and miles of nameless gray lakes. We flew just beneath the low cloud ceiling and in an hour the Yukon came into view. The pilot aligned his plane with the river and flew a short way upstream. From the air the village of St. Mary's appeared to be nothing more than a few small clusters of houses clinging to a hillside.

We dropped suddenly and unevenly, shifting in the strong wind, and touched down with a hard bump. The pilot taxied four hundred yards along the uneven gravel runway. At the end of the runway was a tall hangar with blue metal siding. We came off the airplane. Anna's brother waited for us by the hangar door. The hangar was locked and dark inside.

In the misty air Anna embraced her brother affectionately, pushing hair out of his eyes, and then introduced me as her friend, a medical student from the Lower 48. His face lit up.

"You're a doctor?" he said excitedly.

I explained that I wouldn't be a doctor for many years.

The pilot loaded mail sacks onto the flat bed of the village truck and returned to the plane with an armload of cardboard boxes that would go out through Bethel. Anna's brother piled our bags onto a thick-wheeled ATV. We climbed on behind him and rolled down the hill into the village.

Anna's family had lived in the same prefabricated gov-ernment-issue house for three decades. The house rested on wooden stilts, which held the floor safely above ground while the tundra shifted in its perpetual restlessness. Flakes of paint came off the front of the house. Inside were four rooms: a front living room with a velvety brown couch and black-and-white television, a small kitchen, and in back two bedrooms that six people shared. A room at the side of the house contained two long freezers packed with hundreds of frozen salmon for the winter's eating. The steamy front room had the thick, bitter stench of fish oil. We came into the kitchen, where Anna's mother had put bowls of salmon soup, moose soup, and steamed beaver on a table pushed against the front window. We sat for a while chewing the gristly, smoky meats and fishing oily potatoes out of the stews. The food passed blandly over my tongue and rested heavily in my stomach. Anna said her family ate this same meal every day.

The sky was still bright at nine o'clock when we finished dinner. We walked outside into the cool wet air, and the festive streets were filling with villagers. Women we passed stopped with giddy surprise to hug and kiss Anna and shake her hand, as though she were a local celebrity who had come home. The stoicism and reserve of Yupiks in the clinic and at the hospital had vanished. Children charged down hills at top speed, their cheeks puffing and flushing, to greet us. We drifted into the town hall, a double-wide trailer set on a precipice above the Yukon River. Inside, Anna's sister-in-law twisted streams of pink crepe paper from the ceiling for a cousin's wedding reception the next day. She gestured excitedly toward the decorating plans she had drawn on graph paper.

Later the crowds began to flow toward the new village high school for Friday night's big social event, the fiddling. Outside the high school gym, young people stood smoking in tight clusters, talking with friends and casting inquisitive eyes toward other groups. I followed Anna into the gym, which was steamy with a couple hundred people filling the bleachers.

The basketball hoops had been tethered to the ceiling. On a corner platform, four men in black jeans and tall hats played violins in a bluegrass frenzy. From time to time the fiddlers turned inward to face each other and played together in a chorus, feet tapping and stomping; then one of the violins would catch the fast melody and lift it away from the others, making the music turn and spin and fly. Elders spilled across the basketball court and danced the waltz and two-step. I sat cross-legged on the floor watching the rush and twirl in the room. Anna's father plucked her from the crowd and began to turn her joyfully on the dance floor. When the fiddlers paused, Anna came back sweaty and happy, and we walked outside with Roland and her village friends. She smoked a cigarette languidly, blowing out clouds of stinging smoke. Mosquitoes flew at my forehead and I swatted viciously.

Anna leaned over and said, "If you let them alone, they won't bite." I looked skeptically at her, and her friends giggled. A pilot for one of the regional air companies drew up to the group and recalled 3 a.m. rescue flights to Bethel transporting Anna and the sick patients she had stabilized in the village. He hated those flights with half-mile visibility, wings icing up, cloud ceiling low against the land: three people's lives in danger. I heard the fiddlers start back up again inside and now the faces were coming and going into the brightly lit gym. At midnight I told Anna I was going home, weary from the week. Her friends turned to me in disbelief.

"So early?"

"But the fiddling!"

"Won't you dance?"

I walked back to Anna's house under a cloudy sky brightened by moonlight, up a gravel road and past the darkened town hall, where Anna's cousin would be married tomorrow. Along the way I passed stragglers heading for the gym.

"Aren't you going to the fiddling?"

"I'm going to sleep."

"You're missing the fiddling?"

I let myself in the house and lay awake on the couch for a while. I thought of what I had heard at the hospital—that Anna's family had not wanted her to become a health aide, being female, and then had discouraged her from working. I remembered that Anna had told me over lunch about her failed marriage to a white man. She talked very little about the months that she spent afterward in St. Mary's, husbandless and with a child of mixed race. I had asked if she would ever move back to her home village and she said she would never move back. She smiled and shrugged when I asked why, as she often did when I pressed with my questions.

The house was still when I awoke in the morning, and through the window I stared at deserted gravel streets. The first of Anna's family appeared at noon. I learned they had stayed out dancing until four in the morning, just before the summer sun rose. Together we prepared a breakfast of Spam, eggs, and black coffee. At the table, Anna asked what I wanted to do that day, and I asked if she could take me fishing. I knew the silver salmon were still running and I had heard that people were pulling giant fish out of the river and smoking them on home smokers.

Anna's brother borrowed an aluminum boat in the afternoon

and we headed downstream with her cousins, the boat's seventy-horsepower engine fuming bluish smoke and stinking of gasoline. Hills alongside the river dropped down to a shoreline of tall green grass that looked soft and dewy from a distance. We came ashore where the river bent around and sheltered a pool of calm water. Two of the men took hits off a joint and then one tied a silver spoon to his fishing line and hooked a twenty-inch salmon with a few casual casts. He whooped as the fish slapped the water's surface, and then he shook a fist in the air. We floated into the tall river grass to retrieve his catch. Afterward he sat in the boat smoking cigarettes. We talked very little for two hours, with little action on the water, when the fish suddenly began to bite in earnest. Anna had disappeared onto the high tundra and now moved steadily down the hill, carrying a bucket filled with small firm blueberries wrapped in tight powdery skins. Water had seeped up her boots and pants to the knees and her fingers were stained purple. She chattered excitedly about our catch as she stepped into the rocking boat. I popped a few of the berries into my mouth and they stung sourly on my tongue. My hands and arms were still tremulous from fighting the fish, but I felt a satisfying physical ache from the excitement of the successful hunt.

Later I sat at the kitchen table eating salmon soup with Anna's father, a short, stocky man with a tanned and deeply creased face and Malcolm X–style glasses. He talked about a time forty years ago when as a bachelor he had lived in Anchorage, like Anna had. I asked him what kind of work he had done and he said the Alaska Department of Fish and Game had offered a full-time job, monitoring the state's rivers.

It sounded like the perfect situation for an Eskimo man who had left school after third grade but had decades of knowledge about seasons and fish cycles.

He said he'd turned down the position and returned to St. Mary's to live instead, never taking a formal job. I asked why he'd come home and he looked out to the foggy afternoon while he considered the long-ago decision. He moved his hands several times before he finally spoke.

"Live from ground," he said slowly. We sat watching rain fall against the window. In a while he stood, pushed in his chair, and said he was going to the town hall to play bingo.

Jane McMurtrie, the overnight attending physician in the emergency department, was examining a breathless patient in the main resuscitation room when I came looking for her. The patient sat forward in the gurney, breathing in deep husky gasps. I hovered in the doorway watching her stethoscope move rapidly across the patient's chest and abdomen. Her hands fluttered down at his calves and she gave a great squeeze around his ankles, then she turned to the nurse with her orders for a chest x-ray, steroids, and an inhaled breathing treatment. The nurse had been in motion the whole time and was reaching for an oxygen hose hanging from the ceiling to connect a pipe-shaped device that aerosolized medicine into the patient's lungs. Dr. McMurtrie glanced at the patient again then walked toward me.

"Okay, what do you have?" she said. She had a thin, sharp nose and long hair tied back with a rubber band.

"Twenty-year-old with runny nose and fever . . ."

"Wait." She motioned for me to stop, then strode briskly into the emergency department hallway. I followed her around the far corner and into the stockroom, where she indicated that I sit down. Puzzled, I sat on an unopened box pushed up against the wall. Around the room, shelves were crammed full of rolled tape, bandages, dressings, sheathed needles, IV catheters, blood culture bottles, syringes individually wrapped in plastic.

Dr. McMurtrie sat across from me and said, "Okay, tell me about your patient."

I looked down at notes I'd made in the margin of the double-copy emergency room sheet and began to tell the story in the fashion I'd learned. The patient was a young employee of the fish packing plant who worked in a warehouse cell fourteen hours every day, shoveling frozen fish in twenty-nine-degree air. She took Sundays off. The last couple nights she hadn't slept well due to a stuffy nose. I looked up to see Dr. McMurtrie scrutinizing me and thought I detected a pucker of impatience on her mouth.

"Did she have a fever?"

I looked back down at the sheet.

"Yes, 38.2 degrees C," I said.

"Is that a fever?"

"I think so."

"Let's call 38.5 degrees a real fever," she said. "What else does she have?"

"She has green nasal discharge, a frontal headache, a sore throat, a dry cough, and chills. No shortness of breath, chest pain, nausea, vomiting, or diarrhea."

"Any pertinent past history?"

"She's healthy."

"Does she take any meds?"

"Tylenol for the headache, but nothing else."

"And her exam?"

I reported that I'd triggered pain by pressing over her sinuses, and I described inflamed nasal membranes and swollen lymph nodes under her chin. After talking about the examination I looked up again.

"What do you want to do for her?" Dr. McMurtrie said.

"I was thinking an antibiotic and a decongestant," I said. I had written out the two prescriptions, leaving the bottom blank for an attending doctor's signature, and I was about to pass these to her.

"Alright," Dr. McMurtrie said. "Start from the top, without pausing."

My palms filled with a sudden cold sweat but I was uncertain what could have gone wrong. The patient's story was straightforward, so I didn't think I'd missed anything in the history or exam, and I felt certain my diagnosis and plan were correct. Why would an attending want to go over a case of sinusitis a second time? I repeated the story I'd just told, beginning with the patient's work situation and congestive symptoms, her near-fever and chills, her suggestive headache. I related her exam findings, thinking of the knobby lymph nodes rolling under my fingertips, and gave my diagnosis of sinusitis, to be treated with antibiotics and decongestants. When I finished, Dr. McMurtrie nodded with a faint smile, held up one finger, and said, "One more time."

Flabbergasted now, I ran through the presentation a third time and when I finished she said, "Yes. Good." She repeated the presentation back to me, cutting all nonessentials, and finished in thirty seconds.

"Got it?" she said.

"Yes," I said.

"Work on your presentations," she said. Then I remembered what I had witnessed all along in Bethel: that telling the story was the crucial first step in taking care of a patient. A presentation explained to any doctor what had happened to a patient, what treatment to pursue, and why. If I didn't know what was wrong or what therapy to give, the presentation could be an appeal for help. I was coming to a new place now. I wasn't just observing the human condition, like a photographer making pictures of what people felt and experienced; I had begun evaluating a patient's condition and was learning to speak in an equal language with other doctors. I had become a kind of activist for the sick, telling the story with my voice.

Basic communication within the Bethel emergency department happened at a long chalkboard in the hallway outside the main resuscitation suite. The triage nurse entered every new patient's name and problem onto the chalkboard grid each time a room cleared up, and that's how doctors knew a patient was ready to be seen. Typically the description of the presenting problem was brief; "vomiting" was common, as was "cough." Doctors signed their initials on the board next to the names of patients they took on. From the board I began to cherry-pick my own patients and soon fell to the strategy of choosing one specific complaint each day and seeing only patients with that issue, with the idea of learning by repetition.

One afternoon I selected "cough" as my problem of choice and wrote my initials next to the name Virgil Littlebear. I expected to discover that Virgil had bronchitis or pneumonia, like the majority of patients I'd seen in Bethel who raised such complaints. As I was beginning to see patients with some degree of independence, I would visit with Virgil first to obtain his story and examination, present his case to the attending physician, and then she would meet him.

When I walked into the examination room, Virgil looked up from where he sat on a padded bench, his back against the wall. He had the kind smile of a pacifist and severe cheekbones. He also looked greatly aged for a forty-year-old. His fingers were bony and rested calmly on his thighs. I pulled the chair away from the doctor's desk and positioned myself three feet from Virgil, facing him directly.

Virgil began to describe his situation. He had come that day from his native village of Chevak, a four-hundred-person Eskimo settlement at the mouth of the Kuskokwim River, in a privately hired Cessna. In Chevak, Virgil worked as a mechanic. He told me he had lost weight and had felt profoundly exhausted over the preceding few weeks. He hadn't been dieting. He had lost twenty pounds easy, he said, and never felt hungry anymore. Looking at the loose drape of his shirt at his shoulders and the pooling of pants about his thighs, I wondered if he'd lost a lot more than twenty pounds. He talked about a cough that had nagged for months, that felt lately like it had moved deep down in his chest. Just recently he had experienced fevers and sweats, particularly in the late afternoon and again in the middle of the night. He lived with his mother, a healthy woman who had not suffered any of these ailments. Occasionally he brought up yellow mucus but hadn't seen blood in the phlegm. He knew how that looked, having had tuberculosis as a teenager, when the disease ran rampant through Yupik villages. He'd swallowed a troughful of horse pills for nine months then, and recovered.

After describing the cough at some length, Virgil said he had pain in his stomach, chest, and back. He touched each of the painful areas lightly with his hand, and then he smiled his sad, easy smile. I had seen Yupik women tolerate incredible levels of pain but I did not think right away that Virgil, a Yupik man, might also have more significant pain than he let on.

I mulled over Virgil's symptoms. I felt almost certain he harbored a serious diagnosis, something that might even be fatal. His unintended weight loss concerned me most. Weight loss plus his persistent cough could mean the old tuberculosis had reawakened. Weight loss could have also signified cancer, although with his many complaints I couldn't pinpoint one spot where the cancer might have originated. Inwardly I felt strong resistance to the idea that he had cancer, and in a moment I understood this feeling came from my own not wanting him to have cancer rather than from any basis in fact. The other diagnosis my mind leapt toward was HIV. Now I could feel the warmth of Virgil's body just a few feet away and I felt something inside of me step back slowly from him.

I pressed my lips together and asked Virgil if he was involved in a sexual relationship. He told me he had been with a village woman for several years but they had not had sex recently. He said he had never used injection drugs. I felt my cheeks burning as he answered me gamely. I apologized for asking such intrusive questions and could not manage to explain that I wondered about HIV. I had never suggested this to a patient before, and I thought it might come out like an accusation. Besides, I did not like this sideways means of implying that I had detected something really wrong with him.

When I stood to examine Virgil, he moved to the table with short, fragile steps and lifted himself up. He removed his shirt and I saw that his skin had sunken and tightened between his ribs. I looked into his mouth and in the tiny caves of his ears and eyes. I held my stethoscope to his chest for a long time, my hand resting on his bony shoulder as I listened for sounds between the heartbeats. Nothing unusual there; the heart and lungs sounded normal. I pushed on his abdomen and he grimaced when I felt over his liver, spleen, and lower back.

After I finished the exam, I told Virgil I wanted to discuss his condition with the senior physician and would return in a few minutes to explain what came next. Again he smiled his sad, easy smile. I put on a pleasant face that I hoped did not betray the serious concern I felt.

I went down the emergency department hallway and hoisted myself onto one of the tall stools at the table where doctors wrote their charts. Suddenly all I wanted was a safe classroom and a syllabus and a calm sage who would reveal everything a doctor should know and feel about the human condition.

First I might learn simple, ordinary details of human lives and become acquainted with what a person experiences at thirty, fifty, seventy, ninety years. I could learn about the turmoil of an instantaneous quadriplegia or a diagnosis of cancer, witness the joy of a healthy child, the human body's longevity, and take on the sharp, weathered human mind. At the conclusion of my crash course I would possess a deep appreciation and sympathy for human lives, and I would not be paralyzed by questions of the human heart, as I was at just that moment.

Then I snapped out of my daydream and studied the notes I'd made. In the margin I had written a long list of Virgil's medical problems, which I now began to unscramble and prioritize in my head. I was determined to uncover one diagnosis that could explain every twinge and ache that Virgil experienced.

The on-duty attending was a middle-aged woman from South Africa named Dr. Peabody, who had worked at the hospital for five years. She hung Virgil's chest x-rays on the light board while I related what I had learned. Looking closely, we picked out tiny white dots showered across both lung fields.

"Could those be little . . . tumors?" I asked. I was surprised how hard a time I had verbalizing a word that signified cancer.

Dr. Peabody said, "It could. This could also be miliary tuberculosis." Miliary tuberculosis is a less common form of tuberculosis that looks like sprays of buckshot on a chest x-ray. I did not know yet that miliary disease is one way that tuberculosis reactivates. More commonly, tuberculosis looks like pneumonia or a round cavity at the top of the lung.

"This guy is a walking time bomb," the attending said, and she directed me to perform a rectal exam and check for a prostate nodule. A flash of terror went through me and must have showed on my face, because the doctor and nurse turned toward each other with sudden laughter and then Dr. Peabody said, "Don't worry, you'll get used to it."

I knocked timidly at Virgil's door, went in, and explained what I had to do. Several moments passed with horrifying inevitability. I thought of how I'd done rectal exams only on practice patients and that I'd have no clue if I felt a prostate nodule. Nevertheless, Virgil turned himself over wordlessly. A damp sweat broke out under my arms and in the bends of my elbows, and I could feel a suffocated sweat under the latex gloves that I pulled onto my hands. He dropped his trousers and I saw that his buttocks had wasted down to two sharp ridges of bone. An automatic voice in my head reached to name the bony landmarks and I wondered maddeningly if I had passed the point where I could still turn off that objective, clinical voice that seemed so wrong for the moment.

I remembered hearing an African relief worker say the buttocks are the human body's last reserve and he could predict who was near death by the amount of padding left on a patient's buttocks. I realized that Virgil's weight loss related to breaking down all his muscle and fat, which was keeping him alive but slowly dissolving his body. Trembling and terrified, I performed the uncomfortable exam. I touched the smooth, firm prostate but didn't know if I'd felt anything abnormal. While I washed my hands in the corner, Virgil turned back to the room, looking at the floor, and then I left the room without making eye contact.

In the hallway, Dr. Peabody began talking with me again

about the different things that could be wrong with Virgil, but I was so shaken up by his wasted body that I didn't hear her well. Finally I clicked out of my thoughts when I heard her say, "This guy comes walking down the hall, all skinny like that, he has cancer written all over him."

"We probably can't do much for him," she said. She turned sharply towards Virgil's room and entered. I stood in a corner while she repeated some of the questions I'd asked and then carefully examined his lungs and stomach.

"I don't know what's going on, but we need to find out," she said to Virgil. She explained that testing might yield an answer. She handed him order slips for blood work and additional x-rays and asked if he had questions. He shook his head. She handed me his chart and we filed silently out of the room.

Later in medical school, I would care for terminal AIDS patients in Seattle and again in southern Africa. The dying patients looked like skeletons, with cloudy eyes like ghosts, but few of these patients would look as bad as I remembered Virgil looking. That night while I tried to fall asleep, I turned over visions of his body's horrifying thinness, the taut skin stretched between extruded bony ridges, dark folds under his eyes. Inevitably I would loop back to the thought that he was dying.

Although I'd planned to take the next evening off from hospital work, I stopped by the emergency department hoping to find Virgil's blood test results and to even catch a glimpse of him, to reassure myself that he was still alive. Unfamiliar with the ways of the seriously ill, I expected that he could drop dead at any moment. In the hallway I passed Dr. Peabody, who mentioned that she had examined Virgil's abdomen by ultra-sound that day but had not seen anything abnormal around his pancreas or liver. She said tuberculosis cultures were sent to the state laboratory and results would not be back for several weeks. I looked at his blood tests, which showed platelet and electrolyte abnormalities—all evidence of something wrong—but no conclusive data to back one single diagnosis. An HIV test had still not become available at that remote hospital. So nothing concrete had come of all the tests.

I spotted Virgil in the waiting area and headed toward him. We spoke briefly about the results and avoided talk of what could be wrong. I did not know how to tell him how sick he was. What would he think? What unanswerable questions would he ask? I did not know the right words to address his profound existential issues so instead I said, "We have got to find out what's going on. We have to do more testing." It didn't occur to me that he had likely thought about dying and even believed that he was not long for this world. It didn't occur to me that he might not need every kind of answer from a twenty-three-year-old wearing jeans and a stethoscope. It didn't occur to me that maybe all he wanted right then was simple human contact—that I was doing alright by him.

That evening I told Virgil's story to two family practice doctors working in the emergency department. Despite all the new details, neither arrived at a more specific diagnosis and I felt disappointed, wondering if the story I told had been too vague or if I had neglected to uncover the one crucial piece of information that would give away the diagnosis. Still, I held out hope that the right test could answer his mystery.

Just then I wished I could be magically accelerated through training and snap my fingers to name what ailed him, and tend more fully to his human needs.

Virgil boarded a Boeing 737 bound for Anchorage the next morning, where specialists and sophisticated machines would help determine what was wrong. Because I was returning to Seattle in a week, I understood I would never see him again, and I ached to know I might never hear what became of him. The word in the emergency department hallway the evening before I left was that his testing had still been inconclusive. I wondered how he was thriving in that big-city hospital, suspended in the lonely unknown, and I imagined him walking restless laps up and down the ward to keep up his waning strength. I wondered if he would eat the plain American hospital fare offered him. The plan was for a surgeon to open Virgil's chest that week to remove a lung nodule in hopes of making a biopsy diagnosis.

I departed on the early flight to Anchorage one quiet morning at the beginning of September. As we taxied toward take-off, morning sunlight suddenly hit the tundra and mingled with shadows in the frosty, undulant ground, turning the land a brilliant red gold. Just then I felt the land was inside me, and then I felt I was learning to tell a story that mattered. In the hospital one night, I had written Virgil's test results on the back of an envelope, which I carried home in my bags, hoping to eventually gain clues to his disease. During second year of medical school, I learned hundreds of new diseases and on several occasions took out the envelope and ruminated over his results. I was never able to make much of the laboratory abnormalities, though, and by midyear my memory for him had faded enough that I gave up trying to make the diagnosis.

What remained were a pair of story endings I daydreamed while I roamed the wards at Seattle's county hospital one early spring afternoon. One version held that lymphoma had spread widely through Virgil's body; that he'd remained on the ward in Anchorage the last three weeks of his life, mingled shyly with the native Alaskans hospitalized there, then lay down with morphine trickling through his veins and damping out the excruciating pain in his chest, and died in his sleep. Another version held that he suffered from disseminated tuberculosis; that he embarked on a course of heavyweight antibiotics at the Anchorage hospital and began to sweat out the infection. He flew back to Bethel months later and fifteen pounds heavier, his cheeks filled out from the potato chips he'd gotten hooked on, hauling a heavy bag that held the remainder of a year's antibiotics. In that version, it was no trouble at all to imagine him home in Chevak now, moving easily and heartily in the still, cold land, mending the family's fish nets in advance of the spring harvest, preparing for the salmon runs soon to pass up the muddy Kuskokwim River.

CHAPTER 2

Seattle

———❦———

Fall quarter of second year had a reputation for being the hardest stretch of medical school. Course outlines stacked up to a pile two feet tall, lectures consumed thirty-five hours of the week, and we juggled a load of eight classes, most focused on a single organ system like the lung or heart. I returned from Alaska full of fire to excel in the classroom and reclaimed my perch in the lecture hall, writing copious notes into blank notebooks, one per organ system. Gradually I began to function like a classroom student again and devolved into a primitive machine that ate textbooks and syllabi and spit out answers on multiple-choice exams. The quarter began right after Labor Day, pressed on relentlessly with examinations every Monday morning, and ended in a tidal wave of finals that spanned the two weeks up through Christmas. Thoughts of clinical medicine faded back into an abstraction. I encountered two or three forgettable patients on staged assignments and otherwise didn't set foot in a real clinic or talk with a practicing doctor for months. Bethel felt like a thing of the past.

The Seattle rain set in. I felt impossibly run down after the onerous fall quarter and mustered little enthusiasm for the winter ahead. Class struck up again after the holiday break and I fell back on routines, biking though cold misty mornings to class, slogging through lectures with a *New York Times* crossword puzzle, slipping notes to girlfriends while a famous cardiac physiologist carried on about drugs with designations like FK-506 and McD-323. I ran laps around Greenlake in the early evenings, tackled the books for one or two halfhearted hours, and went out for beer and darts on the weekends with a group of medical students that now included WWAMI arrivals from Idaho, Montana, and Alaska. I got myself romantically entangled with a geology student from Missoula and spent nights chatting about guitars and English poetry with him instead of studying the gastrointestinal tract.

I did not think much about medicine until one sleepy winter morning when third-year scheduling packages arrived in the student mail room and WWAMI popped up again in the form of a medical-student travel adventure . Third year would mark my debut on the hospital wards, the formal start of clinical training, and to my mind, the greatly overdue beginning of patient care. Now I faced delicious choices like the surgery service at a Seattle trauma hospital that cranked through hundreds of gunshot and motor vehicle injuries every month, versus a solo general surgeon in Helena, Montana, who knew just about everyone in town and removed appendixes, gall bladders, and the occasional tumor. The prospect of imminent immersion in the clinical world revived me from sodden hibernation.

A few ground rules pertained to the adventure travel game. Because WWAMI rotations were popular with third-year students, we were to indicate an overall preference for rural sites if that was our wish, and to make doubly sure with requests for specific locales and specialties. A few rotations were particularly sought after. Psychiatry was superb in Anchorage, and as a bonus the site provided a four-wheel-drive vehicle for student weekend ventures. Spokane obstetrics and gynecology offered the greatest prospect of deliveries, and Havre, Montana, a two-day drive from Seattle, was regarded as the best family practice rotation. No single medical student would receive assignments with all the premium sites, but we could make requests and would likely receive one or two of the choice spots if we wished. Students who spent the previous year in the WWAMI states had first pick.

For days the class filled with talk about third-year rotations. Many students from WWAMI-land planned to head straight home when the new academic year began in July; several would spend their entire clinical training in Idaho on primary-care tracks and not pass another unnecessary moment in Seattle. Others were firmly attached to the city and had no interest in venturing to WWAMI-land. One whose sights were trained on academic neurosurgery grumbled particularly about the possibility of not having his laboratory close by. Most students fell somewhere between these extremes and hoped for a moderate dose of WWAMI, with home base in Seattle.

These scheduling choices were the first I would make about my future as a doctor, and the decisions felt momentous. I hoped to become a pediatrician, and picking a pediatric rotation seemed the most crucial decision of all. The following week I visited my mentor at Children's Hospital, a bigwig named Fred Starbuck. Starbuck had been at Children's for two decades and walked scores of medical students through residency and into practice, so I expected to take his direction seriously. He advised unequivocally that the best place to see the daily practice of pediatrics was Pocatello, Idaho, where an old respected group kept a busy clinic and hospital practice. Pocatello had a good reputation among senior medical students and pediatric residents for the same reason, but I wasn't sold on the idea. I worried about being away from the big names at Seattle Children's and wondered whether disappearing to Pocatello would make me invisible when I sought a residency. Starbuck thumped me on the shoulder and said to come back for a specialty rotation at Children's during fourth year and impress the big shots then. Still, I was afraid that southeast Idaho would not be a friendly place for a small Asian woman.

While deliberating, I gave little thought to what would make me into the kind of doctor I hoped to be, or whether I would find my heroes in the midnight bowels of a great city hospital or in a small dusty desert hamlet. For months I had been cooped up with 175 overachievers and worried myself over class rankings and residency letters. I hadn't seen real patients since the summer before or thought about the day-to-day interactions that turned a medical student into a good clinician. Then I recalled Bethel and the fresh and real and gritty medicine I had seen, and I remembered how much I'd enjoyed my patients, co-workers, and neighbors.

In the end I didn't have the guts to turn myself over entirely to the great unknown and like most of my classmates decided on an even mixture of WWAMI and Seattle rotations. If I changed my mind later in the year, I could trade. I inked my preferences, turned in the leafy packet of requests, and lapsed back into the quiet academic winter.

As the year trundled on, I learned to cram from the syllabus on Sundays and pass my exams with a minimum of stress and output. The moment we finished, I skipped town for the dry snowy mountains of Montana. What remains most from that winter was coming to love the solitude of the long road and quiet high-altitude forests and wide flat rivers cutting beneath mountain ranges.

Spring quarter began and passed almost unnoticed. Most evenings at home were boisterous, with classmates frequently stopping by to hang out and to watch the television show ER on Thursday nights, before we all headed to a cafe for an hour or two of brisk studying. I filled my evenings with soccer matches, alternative theater, and dinners and drinks with friends. The interstate romance waned.

Third-year schedules finally appeared in our mailboxes one warm spring morning. Between classes I leapt up the stairs and hurried into the mail room, where classmates were ripping open envelopes. Everyone was eager for classes to end and the wards to begin. I reached into my mailbox and tore out my schedule. For the first six weeks I was assigned to a general surgery team at Harborview, the county hospital in Seattle. I flushed with terror at the thought of tyrannical surgeons, interminable hours in the operating room, and sleepless thirty-six hour shifts. I read that psychiatry would follow surgery, and for locale I had drawn the Harborview wards again. After psychiatry, I would rotate to a quiet private hospital in suburban Seattle for obstetrics and gynecology. Next on the list was pediatrics in Pocatello, Idaho, to take me up through Christmas.

I had requested Pocatello as my highest priority in the end, after all my deliberating. Seeing the assignment typed out in black and white, I worried again that I'd made a mistake. Even if Pocatello was the best choice for my potential future in pediatrics, I wondered if I'd like being invisible for weeks, eight hundred miles from Seattle. Maybe I'd go stir-crazy holed up in that arctic WWAMI-land weather, like some of my classmates had during first year, and maybe I'd find I absolutely could not live in a town with one lousy ethnic restaurant, no bookstores to speak of, and not even ESPN. Had the travel adventure gone sour?

As I shuttled back down the stairs to class, I told myself that I would find unexpected satisfactions in the early Pocatello winter, just like I had on the Yupik tundra. I calmed down and decided I'd need a warmer jacket and snow tires. Maybe I would like being called Doc around town and enjoy acquainting myself with families who lived humbly and sparely and with great pride. Maybe I'd come to feel kinship with those whose lives depended upon the plow, upon coal in the ground. Maybe I already understood that I was going to glimpse ribbons of human living I could never have dreamed up.

And then the days stretched to an arctic length, second year tumbled to a close, we holed up and studied frenetically for the first section of the licensing boards, and the warm sweet summer arrived.

Beyond the merest week break, the great unknown of third year loomed.

Chapter 3

Spokane

A t nine o'clock on my first morning in the surgery wards at Seattle's Harborview Hospital, I learned I would be on call that night and wouldn't leave the hospital for more than thirty hours. I had brought my toothbrush just in case. In the ladies' locker room adjoining the operating suites, I changed into a pair of scrubs and donned a new white coat, then met the junior resident in the emergency room where she was evaluating incoming trauma patients. My stylish shoes made my feet ache by dinnertime and a housemate came to the rescue with clean sneakers that I wore through the sleepless night and second workday.

I had never been on my feet so much in my life. Soon I learned my way around the hospital and became practiced in basic surgical skills. I sewed the torn scalps of homeless men and the wrists of suicidal teenagers. My hands felt dozens of bellies and learned the tense feel of an abdomen full of disease that surgeons take to the operating room for further exploration. I started to talk in the sleek and efficient language of medicine and knew more medical facts than ever before.

I was the absolute novice and bottom dweller in the surgical hierarchy, and when I wasn't searching for gauze bandages or taking out sutures in the clinic, I was holding thick metal retractors in the operating room while residents labored through endless surgeries. The interns, who had just graduated from medical school a month earlier and were starting the first of many years of residency training, provided the closest guidance on moment-to-moment issues on the wards. A third-year resident who crawled out of the operating room now and then was in charge of the interns, and a chief resident oversaw the entire clinical service. The attending physician supervised our activities more remotely and interacted mostly with the chief resident. We buffed and polished our surgical knowledge in every spare moment, batting about medical questions on floor rounds, in teaching conferences, on the elevator, and at the operating room sink while scrubbing down to the elbows with foamy brown soap. We quizzed each other while waiting for patients to arrive by ambulance in the emergency room or on the ward from the emergency room. I learned to tell lush scientific stories about the way diseases smoldered, then exploded into being and overran internal organs, and I started to dream in the language of the hospital.

My appearance began to evolve. At work I wore a stiff, white, waist-length coat and carried a pager that summoned me to the emergency department when a big trauma was expected or a case for the general surgeons arrived. My skirts fell below the knee and I wore nylon stockings and closed-toe shoes. I wore scarves to look more distinguished and mature and to disguise the same plain shirts and khaki pants I wore most days. I almost bought clogs.

Something in this metamorphosis rendered me suddenly visible within the medical world. In hospital hallways, families stopped me to ask about patients' conditions and prognoses. They wondered why and how long and when could they go home. "In your experience, how bad is this?" patients asked. It pained me to reply that I couldn't speak from experience.

The surgery rotation ended after six fast weeks and I moved over to the county psychiatry warrens, which included two floors of locked wards in the hospital and the quiet communal inpatient center across the street. The action turned suddenly sedentary. Treatment breakthroughs came while I sat in a deep sofa chair, talking with patients under the glow of muted reading lamps. All day I absorbed stories of childhood abuse, drug addiction, jail time, hallucinations, and suicide attempts. My simmering wish to leave Seattle became gaping desire. After a weekend in the mountains, I began asking around if anyone would trade me their obstetrics rotation; I didn't care so much where, as long as I could leave Seattle. Through a housemate I heard of an Idaho student who'd been apart from her girlfriend for three months and wanted to trade Spokane for Seattle. In minutes, the deal was done.

Now I packed my car with clothes, textbooks, and stereo and fit my dismantled road bike onto the backseat. I said goodbye to housemates on a rainy Sunday afternoon and drove through downtown and veered onto Interstate 90 going east past the suburbs, up into the Cascade Mountains and over Snoqualamie Pass. East of the mountains the air turned balmy. Sunshine and desert terrain and occasional signs of civilized life came in the car windows and in two hours I crossed the Columbia River at Vantage, where it flows wide and flat, and I watched the river meander into the gorge through vast red and orange canyons that shot hundreds of feet into the broad sky. The highway turned on a northeastern incline and pointed toward Spokane, some three hundred road miles from Seattle. I fought the hypnotic fatigue of the straight road by reading aloud from signs that named farm crops planted along the highway and I wondered how I would like Spokane, a city of 300,000 known for conservative politics. Gazing at endless miles of farmland, I realized how isolated the city would be, and I remembered having heard friends born and raised in Spokane describe how they had "escaped."

Then I thought of how within days I would deliver babies while an attending looked on, and this prospect suddenly energized me. I'd listened carefully to my housemate's reports from Spokane obstetrics and had come to believe that delivering babies was a particularly doctor-like thing to do. With obstetrics in my arsenal, I could make a plausible claim to skeptical friends and family that I was finally learning something doctorly. Delivering babies had a much loftier ring, anyway, than tying stitches on drunks who passed out on the church steps and split open eyebrows.

In the cool morning, I drove from the medical student apartment to the hospital just down the hill. A teaching gynecologist showed me and two other students how to operate the office computers, pointed to textbooks and journals we might reference during the rotation, and passed out a basic syllabus with maps of Spokane. The clinic I was assigned to was circled in pen and I saw that I would be ten miles out of town in the rapidly expanding Spokane Valley. The route from the apartment to the clinic was drawn in pink highlighter. The thought came to me that I had never known a pregnant woman or touched a newborn baby, and I felt the world a strange and unknown place again. Just outside the office door were real people whose lives I would enter in a role that now blurred observation, study, comforting, and healing. I had lost my naivete over the depth of human illness and suffering. I had felt scars on bodies and struggled to pull up those who had fallen in the abyss of mental illness. But now I was beginning new again.

I knew before meeting Sheila that hers would be the first childbirth I witnessed, and knowing this made me shy to meet her. Her room was calm with late afternoon sunlight falling through the tall windows but there was a palpable sense that something big was about to happen. Sheila sat on a soft rumpled quilt spread on the bed and wore a blue hospital gown with the words "Hospital Property" stamped across the chest. Her husband, Rick, sat in a chair beside her. I shook her hand across her swollen belly. From the data sheet in her chart I had learned this was Sheila's first pregnancy, that she'd attended prenatal care faithfully and sailed through her term save for the usual morning sickness. Upturned cards from a pinochle game were spread across the table and a vase of white roses bloomed on the bedside stand. Rick gathered up and shuffled cards while Sheila talked happily of how they planned to have three kids in all. She personally couldn't wait for the day they would pack up the children and get back to the rivers and mountains.

"It's been hard getting around the last couple months," she said.

"We're fly fishermen," Rick said, nodding.

Sheila's eyes turned fresh and warm as she talked about

meeting Rick on a blind date arranged by the church pastor. Within weeks they decided they were right for each other. She pushed a damp lock of hair behind her ears and I saw the grace in her hands and wrists. Two IV bags hung beside her bed and drugs ran into her to augment contractions and knock back the pain. A tocometer, the obstetrician's version of the seismograph, beat rhythmically at her bedside, amplifying the baby's rapid heartbeat and scratching her contractions onto an endless strip of graph paper. The contractions came seven minutes apart.

The conversation paused. I explained that I was a medical student learning obstetrics and asked permission to stay for her daughter's birth. Sheila nodded graciously. I stepped out of the room and went searching for Lucy, the family practice resident who was supervising and teaching me obstetrics. Lucy was reading in the doctor's lounge.

"Great, you met Sheila," Lucy said. "Have you been in a delivery yet?"

I told her no and we started talking of things that would happen when Sheila's cervix dilated fully and she started to push the baby out. Lucy held up a plastic model of the pelvis and a battered Raggedy Ann doll that had been lying on the table, to demonstrate how the baby stretched and turned through the birth canal, the choreography precise and efficient, with a minimum of necessary movements. I repeated the turns back to her so I would remember and think of the steps during Sheila's delivery.

Then Lucy's pager rang, the beeps escalating impatiently in pitch. When she hung up the phone she said, "Sheila's complete." She tossed the plastic pelvis and doll onto the table and we walked down the hall to Sheila's room. The floodlights had been dimmed and Sheila's sister and parents were standing beside the bed, facing her. Rick stood next to her, rubbing her pale thigh. Sheila breathed in restless, shallow puffs as the contractions came on. Nurses broke the bed apart and refashioned the pieces into a chair, forcing Sheila to sit upright. The quilt was folded and stowed in a cabinet. Sheila held her legs apart unnaturally, encouraged by the nurse's firm hands, to give the baby's head additional room to descend. She closed her eyes as contractions came on and Rick counted slowly as she breathed in long, controlled sighs.

Lucy stood at Sheila's feet saying, "Good, good, that's the way." Sheila no longer seemed aware of the flow of doctors and nurses coming and going through the room. Then a hand reached behind the bed and damped the floodlights so darkness fell suddenly and voices in the room hushed. The nurse lit a spotlight and adjusted the arm so the hot bright light shone on Sheila's bare vagina.

Sheila pushed out ten deep grunting contractions over the next half-hour, and I imagined the baby dropping farther and farther through the birth canal, arching her neck to inch around the pelvic bones, holding her pose while the womb relaxed. The tocometer churned out yards of paper into a chaotic pile beside the bed, recording the rise and fall of the contractions.

Suddenly the attending doctor, Dr. Bragg, pushed aside the curtain. A nurse closed the door behind him. Dr. Bragg was short, serious, and clean-shaven. He muttered hello to Sheila and then was at the sink washing with the rapid movements of the surgeon who feels great confidence in his hands. Dr. Bragg was a specialist in women's cancers in addition to being an obstetrician and when I assisted him with surgeries later in the rotation, I found that he operated with seamless speed and grace and with a dancer's fluidity. Unlike most surgeons, he refrained from telling jokes and boasting of his heroic surgeries, and he liked to listen to operas as he worked, so I found his operating room very pleasant, and he was technically beautiful to watch.

Now Dr. Bragg pushed his arms carefully into the sleeves of a sterile blue gown, spinning once so a nurse could tie the gown at the back of his neck. As he plunged hands into his gloves, snapping the latex once on each side, the baby's swollen pink scalp became visible to the world. Sheila's face suddenly filled with pain and anxiety, and she hyperventilated twice and vomited into a plastic basin. Lucy reached down with a gloved hand and pressed against the baby's scalp as the infant began to emerge, blue and limp, covered with a cheesy substance, her shoulders bruising Sheila's vagina and sliding into Lucy's iron grasp. Clear fluid followed the baby out in a rush and splashed on the floor. Dr. Bragg had been standing a few steps back, watching critically as Lucy murmured encouragement to Sheila and skillfully coaxed the baby out. Now he reached in swiftly to clamp and cut the thick white umbilical cord.

Lucy passed the infant to Dr. Bragg, who laid her on his forearm and suctioned her throat roughly. The infant's eyes were shut tightly and her head had swollen into a cone shape from the narrow passage. He slapped her chest several times and tipped her head to the floor, bouncing her on his forearm. She still had not moved. An urgent quiet fell in the room and only the lonely noise of the doctor's gloved hand thumping the infant's body sounded through the dark stillness. *She looks dead*, I thought urgently, searching Dr. Bragg's expression for any glimmer of news. Rick stood on tiptoes, looking over the doctor's hunched shoulders. Sheila's eyes were flung wide open and unblinking, watching the spectacle at her feet. The snow-white umbilical cord still hung out of her, the clamp attached to the free end and swinging rudely over the floor. Someone leaning against the back windows exhaled loudly.

"She's a girl," the doctor said.

Then the baby's arm jerked and she gasped and the doctor passed her quickly to a nurse waiting at the incubator. Finally the infant bleated in the quiet room and took two weak cries. She paused a long moment, then began crying forcefully. Cheers rose from Sheila's parents and spread to Rick and the nurses and finally to Lucy and the attending doctor, who clapped with his bloody gloves. Rick turned to shake his father-in-law's hand and swooped down to embrace his mother-in-law. I hadn't moved from Sheila's side, and I stood wordlessly digesting what I'd just seen.

Dr. Bragg's expression turned taut again and he instructed me to press on Sheila's tender belly, massaging the uterus. I touched Sheila's deflated abdomen, felt the tense organ float up beneath my fingers, and pushed gingerly, afraid to prolong her pain. She was shivering uncontrollably from the adrenaline storm that followed birth, and I felt a chill go through me.

"You really need to crank down on that uterus," Dr. Bragg

said, shaking his head, moving beside me and pushing roughly on my hands so I could feel what he wanted. Sheila groaned, clutching a bedrail with her left hand and the mattress in her right hand.

Lucy tugged on the umbilical cord, urging the placenta through the birth canal and directing it into a silver basin I held. The placenta had the shape of a giant kidney bean, and rays of blood vessels gripped the surface membrane. I leaned close to the hot white light, examining this creature. Suddenly I could smell the puddles of blood and amniotic fluid congealing on the floor and I felt faint.

Bright blood trickled from Sheila's vagina while I tried to regain my bearings. Dr. Bragg pressed back on her labia and pointed to where the baby's shoulders had scratched and torn Sheila's flesh during the birth. He blotted pooling blood to show the extent of the cuts. Lucy clicked a curved needle onto the suture instrument and drew lidocaine into a syringe. She injected the tissue, then began pulling stitches through the jagged cut. Sheila had slumped down in bed like a gutted fish, oblivious to the activity and mutterings at her feet.

When everything ended at two o'clock in the morning, I stumbled out to the hall and back to the doctor's lounge by the newborn nursery. An infomercial for an indoor cross-country ski machine played loudly on television, and I snapped off the power on my way past. In the dark room I closed my eyes, which burned with salt and irritation, and thought briefly of what the textbooks described and what Lucy had showed me earlier, the way the infant turns ninety degrees and comes through the birth canal, admitting shoulders one by one. I rehashed the anatomy of the placenta, and the pattern of stitches to repair tears made by the baby. I heard Dr. Bragg walk into the room next door and dictate Sheila's delivery in a muffled voice, and then I heard the closing of the door followed by silence.

I replayed in my mind how the gray, mottled infant had torn noiselessly through the birth canal, leaving a bloody wake behind. I thought of the wash and spray that rushed out after the placenta, which had seemed so shocking and extra-terrestrial, and how everything had splashed down into the metallic basin. For a moment I smelled the acidic stink in the room again and my stomach turned. Later I would identify the smell as amniotic fluid and smell the fluid on my scrubs and in my hair, and in the steam of a shower after a long night in the hospital.

I thought of the silence while waiting for the infant to breathe, her body numb and still.

I curled up and tried to make myself believe I would get used to these discomforts. I felt I ought to push aside my quea-siness with birth, with infants breathing sluggishly, with amni-otic fluid. I had almost fainted during a brief surgery once in Bethel, colors fading around me and gray spots sparkling at the edge of my visual fields like out-of-focus pixels on a televi-sion screen. Suddenly the world had narrowed to a tunnel and all the noise of the room had disappeared and then I sat with my head between my knees, awake again. I had been mortified by that near-fainting and had made myself recover quickly; I never swooned again in Bethel or during the dozens of surger-ies I observed and assisted with at the county hospital.

Now, in my early morning exhaustion, I told myself that

doctors did not stand to the side feeling faint and ill at the sight of bleeding. Doctors could see through their uneasiness and offer comfort for anxious parents and husbands and sick patients. I was going to be a doctor, and doctors took care of sick people. Doctors were strong.

I lay awake for some time beholding images of birthing.

I forced myself to visit Sheila a day later, despite misgivings about my reactions in the delivery room, and again I stepped shyly into her room, as though she were a celebrity I had chanced to meet. Sheila recognized me and smiled warmly. In her face I saw she had finally slept a deep and full night's sleep, and I watched the baby doze on her stomach. She thanked me for helping at the delivery and I stood uncertainly for a moment, not quite sure how to respond. Finally I mumbled thanks of my own. She glanced down demurely at the baby. A light came into her eyes and everything was right in the world.

As hoped, my squeamishness with the onerous sights and smells of birth quickly faded back. A few days after Sheila's delivery, the hospital operator announced my name overhead, calling me to the obstetrics ward. When I arrived in the patient's room I was guided to the sink then briskly shepherded into a blue paper gown and given thick long latex gloves to wear. The nurse stationed me at the mother's feet where I could already see the infant's scalp, covered in matted hair. Immediately I was overtaken with worry that I wouldn't be able to perform the hand movements that I could recite perfectly from memory. An attending obstetrician stood beside me and moved my hands with his so I would do the right things in my nervous stewardship of the infant, shoulder by shoulder, into the world. He turned towards the door and said so softly that it might have been my imagination, "Whatever you do, you cannot drop the baby."

I caught the infant as he slipped forward and landed in my arms like a trout jumping from a river. After we finished the mother's repair and the nurses packed up and shipped the baby to the newborn nursery, I retreated to the couch in the doctor's lounge, turned on the nightly news, and practiced the hand movements until they felt elegant. I told myself I had overcome a setback simply by showing up for work and plugging along gamely.

I was also coming up to speed in the maternity clinic, where I visited with patients who had recently become pregnant. The women were generally healthy despite being pale with nausea, and on the whole the cases were straightforward with minimal decision-making required.

The afternoon's new patient was a teenager named Sara Birch, and she looked with intense scrutiny at me when I walked in. With further experience I learned to recognize this look as mistrust for doctors, but being new to the game, I did not catch on until she began telling her story. Sara wore a blue jeans jacket over thick black sweats, and old tennis shoes. Her hands were curled loosely in fists, and she had silver rings on each of her fingers, giving the appearance of brass knuckles. Her face was puffy and pale with a long thin nose, and she chewed her gum methodically. I smiled brightly, aware of my long skirt swaying as I turned and sat down, and I felt glad to have worn my white coat. I placed Sara's thin, stiff chart on the desk and opened to the four-page data sheet that I would begin to fill out, to leave a record of her pregnancy for the doctors, residents, and students who would care for her at various points of her pregnancy and later deliver her baby.

"I'm so sick," Sara said, as soon as I was seated.

"Sorry to hear that," I said. "When are you due?"

"I don't know," she said. She snapped her gum twice.

I asked about her last period and reached into the pocket of my white coat for a pregnancy wheel that a pharmaceutical rep had given me, the name of the birth control pills he promoted stamped in lavender letters across the middle of the wheel. Matching the date of her period with the grid on the wheel, I saw that she was fifteen weeks along and would deliver in February.

"A Valentine's baby," I said. I wrote the expected date of delivery at the top of the data sheet.

"Is this the first time you've been to a doctor about being pregnant?" I asked.

Sara pressed her lips together and after a moment said, "Yes."

I held a neutral expression.

"Not that I didn't try," she said.

I put the wheel back in my pocket, crossed my legs, and looked at her. She had gorgeous red curls gathered up into a ponytail, heavy black eyeliner, and long eyelashes that curled up against her eyelids.

"I just came from Texas," she said. "My dad lives there. My mom died when I was seven." When she told the baby's father that she was pregnant, he said, "You're lying." He thought she was trying to get money from him. She never told her father.

"I always wanted to be married before having children,"

she said. "But I don't believe in abortion. Things don't always work out the way you plan."

On the morning she took off with a duffel bag of clothing, makeup, and her driver's license, she wasn't feeling well. A friend drove her to Arkansas and she tried to see a doctor in Little Rock for the flu. Over the phone, a woman with a slow drawl told her the schedule was booked but if she waited out the weekend, she could come in on Monday. Before Monday, she made her way to southern Illinois with two boys heading back to college and from there planned to hop a bus to Washington state where her aunt lived. Soon she was vomiting everything she ate and vomiting even when she stopped eating. In the humid, hundred-degree weather she became sluggish and dizzy. She found the closest doctor's office. At the front desk a receptionist with stylish square glasses turned her away.

"I don't have insurance," she said.

She sat in the doctor's waiting room and threw up several times in the trash can. The receptionist asked her to leave and Sara said she wouldn't leave until she talked to the doctor.

"I made the patients in the waiting room really nervous," she said, her voice becoming bold and hard. "I sat there all day throwing up. I had to see that doctor." Finally the patients in the waiting room took up a collection for her and one man wrote a check to the clinic. At the end of the day the doctor saw her and gave her fluids through an IV.

She had arrived in Spokane the previous week and now lived at her aunt's apartment, where she slept on a hideaway bed in the spare room. She still got sick every day and had lost fifteen pounds.

"If it was normal circumstances, I'd be happy to lose fifteen pounds," she said.

After I finished talking to Sara, I went to the back room and sat with the attending physician, Dr. Murray, talking about Sara's case. I mentioned that she had come from Texas and that a whole trimester of pregnancy had passed without medical attention. I said she had been vomiting excessively. I did not mention the trash can or the receptionist with the square glasses. He asked what I thought the problem was. I said we wanted to make certain she didn't have a fetal tumor and the baby was healthy.

Dr. Murray agreed and went into the room pulling the ultrasound machine behind him. Sara scrutinized him intensely when he came in behind me.

"Have you had an ultrasound before?" he asked.

Sara looked at me. "Did you tell him?" she said, crossing her arms.

"He knows," I said.

"Some women do get this ill just from morning sickness," he said. He explained what he was going to do and then pressed the wand of the ultrasound against her belly. The snowy image of the fetus came up, large head bobbing in and out of sight. Dr. Murray touched the screen where the fetus's chest flickered in the center like a candle flame.

"Do you know what that is?" he asked.

"No way," Sara said, breaking into a grin. "That's the heart."

I felt a small quake of happiness inside, hearing the tenderness in her voice.

"All of the parts are there," Dr. Murray said. He flipped the handle of the ultrasound to show the baby's arms and spine and then a foot. "Everything looks just fine in there."

A blood sample confirmed that Sara's pregnancy was in good order and that her vomiting was simple morning sickness. I told Sara what Dr. Murray had coached me to say: that for most women, morning sickness mostly resolves by the second trimester; that we had no good medicine for vomiting, but sometimes small meals helped, bland food, carbonated drinks. She nodded and smiled as I talked.

"I feel a lot better already," Sara said.

"Sorry you've had such a hard time," I said.

"Thanks for letting me vent," she said. In her hand she held the ultrasound picture that Dr. Murray had printed from the machine.

After work I walked to the hospital cafeteria and ate dinner with two medical students in rotation with me at the obstetrics practices in Spokane. We talked about pregnant teenagers we'd seen in our clinics, casually one-upping each other with our stories. I described a gorgeous sixteen-year-old who'd dropped acid during the first trimester, and I heard about a thirteen-year-old who didn't realize for seven months that she was pregnant and a nineteen-year-old already laden with two kids, who now carried a third and was single and jobless. We shook our heads; how could that mother raise all those children without home support or income? We talked of teenage boyfriends who showed affection through put-downs, and absent boyfriends who had walked away before the first home pregnancy tests came back positive. Our quick consensus was that pregnant

61

teenagers had chosen poorly; after all, our types had postponed childbearing until medical school or residency training finished, when we would be in our late twenties or mid-thirties. In our world view, babies were born perfect and deserved stable, mature parents and lives of unlimited possibility.

I wanted to tell Sara's story but thought I could only make her sound like another flaky, irresponsible child. We would have heartily criticized someone reckless enough to get pregnant, flee home, and hitchhike across the country. The fact was that I *liked* Sara. Somewhere in her string of bad decisions was something gritty and determined, something that spoke to reality and survival. I thought of her seated in back of an air-conditioned sedan flying along Missouri highways, college boys up front talking about girls they hoped to date and classes they would take. I imagined her staring vacantly across the wide, flat, fallow land thinking about a new start for herself and the baby. Sara seemed so unequivocally human, so specifically *American*, with her need to right past wrongs and seek a better life. Maybe we were the first to open the door to that second shot at life, and this explained her easy conversion from grumbling to pleased patient. Maybe we had given her the first small piece of that dream, conjuring up the swimming image on the ultrasound screen.

More and more I found myself on unfamiliar ground, in situations wholly outside the experiences of my life. I still didn't believe that teenagers really wanted to have children and I felt emotionally remote from women with difficult cancers or complicated pregnancies. My instinct with these patients was to put on a sterile demeanor and talk about the scientific issues of their conditions in the same hard manner as my attending doctors. But behind that front I continued to take in and process the subtleties of my patients' lives.

One morning in maternity clinic, a nurse handed me a chart and said, "She's here for lab results." I opened the chart to the middle to look at the obstetrical data sheet. The patient's name was Carol Foster, and she had reached the midway point in her pregnancy. From the chart I learned the first parts of her complicated history. She had had her fallopian tubes tied into a knot in her mid-twenties, following a tedious divorce. When she remarried, a surgeon had gone in to reconnect the severed tubes in hopes that the new couple would be able to have children. There had been much uncertainty about whether the procedure would work, but the couple conceived not long after the surgery.

Several printouts were attached to the front of Carol's chart and now I looked at these. Two ultrasound pictures showed a normal-appearing fetus. Someone had circled the fetal spinal cord at the level of his neck. Looking closely at the measurements, I noticed that the size of the spinal cord was slightly above normal range. Not knowing about large spinal cords, I flipped to the next sheet, which contained several bar graphs. One graph was labeled "estriol" and another "alpha-fetoprotein." I did not know what these graphs meant specifically and finally skipped to the last page where the summary statement said the chances of the child having Down syndrome were 1 in 166. So I understood.

I leaned against the wall for a minute, thinking of how to

explain what I had just seen. When I came into the room my hands turned clammy and I wondered, shaking her hand, if I had given away the news already and in a manner that I could not buffer with information and comfort. Carol was a tall woman wearing a taupe pantsuit with black polka dots. By profession she was a sixth-grade teacher, and she loved watching children assert their first independent thoughts. She had deep smile lines that moved as she talked.

"Well, what did we find out?" Carol asked, shifting toward me. She tapped manicured nails twice, rapidly, against the seat.

I held the chart up and moved next to her to show the pictures and graphs.

"On the ultrasound, the baby had a thick spinal cord," I said.

"Right," she said quickly. "I remember. And there was something about his face."

I lifted snowy pictures of the fetus in profile and pointed to the bar graphs.

"Here they measured the pregnancy proteins in your blood," I said, speaking slowly, as I thought of the words. "Some of the proteins were higher than normal."

We sat quietly together looking at the stark graphs, the way the black bars labeled "patient" stood tall and grim next to the petite, slim "normal" bars. I rested my hand on the bottom of the page, not wanting her to see the concluding remarks that I had read.

"So what this all means is that the baby has a very small chance of having Down syndrome," I said finally. Then I mumbled, "About a 1 in 166 chance." Carol took the sheets from me. She had fallen very quiet.

Finally, she said uneasily, "That sounds like maybe, maybe not."

When the attending doctor came in, he said sternly, "This does not mean the baby has got Down's." He urged Carol to obtain chromosome tests to establish whether the baby was truly affected. Chromosomal tests helped women decide whether to continue or to terminate the pregnancy. These terminations were the only kind of abortions performed at private clinics in Spokane.

"We already decided. We're keeping the baby," Carol said, her voice strong again.

We did not talk about what Down's might mean and I felt a cool static creep into the conversation. Carol might have already witnessed some of the problems Down's kids faced, being a primary school teacher and maybe having worked in special education during her career. The most serious complications ran through my mind now: the 25 percent chance of dying from heart failure at one year, the truncated intestines that ended abruptly after the stomach or somewhere in the long, anonymous middle, the severe mental retardation and occasional seizures. I could barely meet Carol's gaze when she went out the door.

Afterward I sat in the back office, mulling over the chart note I would write to summarize Carol's visit. I was having difficulty coming up with words that would dignify her situation. For a while I thought of how I'd fumbled with her lab results. Maybe I should have waited for the attending doctor, who had punted Carol's problem a little farther along the science trail. I thought of how I hadn't wanted to tell her the imprecise results and had wished I could deny any bad news at all to this lovely woman who so dearly wished for motherhood. Now I felt sure we had left her with diminished hopes, that we'd struck down the brilliant life she'd imagined for her new family.

I never heard what came of the chromosome tests or how Carol's baby turned out; that was the drawback of moving from town to town as third-year students did. By the time Carol delivered, I was working with the Pocatello pediatricians and was helping to care for a tiny Down's baby with heart failure. She was beautiful and was trying to gain weight for heart surgery. From time to time I thought of Carol and eventually realized that she would have to quit teaching to give proper care to a Down's baby. It saddened me that she might have to choose such a thing.

Later I saw her choices reflected in a story that my mentor, Dr. Starbuck, told me about a patient from his obstetrics rotation in medical school. The mother had known long before her pregnancy came to term that the child would be stillborn. Ultrasound images showed that the baby had developed without a brain but remained alive in the womb. The pediatrician remembered the horror of seeing the infant's swollen face at delivery, the gaping hole in his skull like the aftermath of a land mine. The umbilical cord was cut. Then to his utter amazement, the mother lifted the baby in her hands, looked at him with the greatest tenderness, and lowered him into her arms as he turned blue and then gray and then died.

In another life, Father Murray had worn the Jesuit priest's robe and celebrated Sunday mass for congregations noisy with children in one of the vast agricultural valleys of south-eastern Oregon. He had taken a vow of poverty at the age of twenty-one and driven farmland backroads in a gray Chevy truck, baptizing infants, praying with tense families, blessing the dead. Priesthood helped him serve his passion for being with people in desperate times. He found his work lifted that desperation sometimes, and this brought him great joy.

Fifteen years later, Father Murray was living in Spokane and had been remade into a family doctor. He lived sparely in a small house on the hill behind the hospital and continued to abide by his Jesuit vow of poverty. Before a day of seeing patients, we sat in his office talking about his practice. He was a lanky man, six feet tall, and wore his silvery hair cut cleanly and conservatively. Prominent glasses distorted and enlarged his blue eyes. He wore a plum-colored wool sweater, the sleeves folded neatly, once, at the wrists. He had an air of tranquility about him.

After a few sentences of small talk, he sat up, ramrod straight, and turned to me with his magnified eyes. He said very slowly, "No one should be denied health care."

"That is the hospital's mission," he added.

When I did not respond, he said, "I tell students and residents that while you work in my clinic, you have to be a democrat. Yes? So you are a democrat today."

I nodded, and he began to describe his work at the hospital's free clinic for pregnant women. The clinic took in anyone who did not have health insurance or could not afford to see a regular obstetrician. Most women who landed in the clinic's net were teenagers. Some were homeless. Some had addictions to heroin or cigarettes, or drank in weeklong binges. Many had dropped out of high school, and rarely did the baby's father stay in the picture. The doctor said he opposed abortion and believed he provided an alternative. I nodded again. I had only met one patient who was visibly unhappy with her pregnancy—she had checked three home tests, all of which had turned positive—and we had filled in her data sheet, prescribed prenatal vitamins, and told her to come back in six weeks for an ultrasound. One of the obstetricians across town had told me that none of the private doctors in Spokane did abortions on demand. He said that abortions were lucrative if you were willing to perform them, because the women paid cash on the spot, hundreds of dollars per. Patients went to Yakima Planned Parenthood to end pregnancies, he said. Yakima was 150 miles down the interstate.

Now Dr. Murray said, "By the time they reach term, eighteen of twenty of our patients will have insurance, and this helps to pay for the care of all of our women. We help them get that insurance.

"That is not why we do this, to make money. Yes?" He smiled wryly.

Across the hallway he showed me the "laboratory," a small room with a microscope pushed against the wall and brown particleboard cabinets filled with boxes of swabs, speculums, and syringes. The parts of a crude ultrasound device, to divine and amplify a fetal heartbeat, were piled on a table. The clinic was designed with now out-of-date elements: thin olive-colored carpets, glossy yellow Formica countertops, hollow brown doors that swung weightlessly on hinges. I knew conversations could be heard through such doors. When I took everything in, I saw how starkly the free clinic contrasted with the private offices, which were furnished with patterned pink wallpaper and blooming flowers and comfortable cotton gowns for the patients.

Dr. Murray lifted a chart off the table and said, "This is Amanda Brady, sixteen years old."

This was Amanda's first pregnancy and she was close to term. Dr. Murray turned to the data sheet at the center of her chart and pointed to where it showed that she had smoked marijuana and binged on beer through the first four months, unaware of being pregnant. An ultrasound exam done not long after she had established herself at the clinic had shown a small fetus. On her data sheet, the "pregnancy desired?" and "partner supportive?" boxes had been left blank.

"She's pretty typical of our clientele," he said. We went into her room together. Amanda sat cross-legged on the exam table and wore an oversize sweatshirt pulled over her round belly. Her hair was wispy and drawn up into a knot at the back of her head. She looked as though she hadn't showered in a few days. Her eyes tracked Dr. Murray as he crossed the room.

"How are you doing, Amanda?" Dr. Murray said, touching her knee.

"I'm down to five smokes a day, but I just can't quit," she blurted out. She clapped a hand over her mouth.

"If I quit for a day, I double my smokes the next day," she said. She sighed noisily.

"You could sprinkle the tobacco on your cereal. You could

put it in your peanut butter and jelly sandwiches," Dr. Murray said. He sat, back straight, on the doctor's stool. "It would be better for kiddo."

Amanda giggled and twisted on the table. I felt my irritation growing.

Then Amanda said "I'm really worried," and she blinked.

She said that she had left her mother's house the previous week and been foraging in garbage bins for scraps of meals. A few days ago she had smelled cat litter on her clothes, known instantly that she had stepped in the stuff while kicking around garbage, and remembered helplessly that she was to avoid cats until she'd delivered the baby.

"Where are you staying?" Dr. Murray said.

"Oh, it depends," she said. "Tonight, at my friend's house. But I couldn't stay at Mom's. I had to get out of there."

She touched her belly with thin, nearly blue hands. "Is he going to get toxo?" she asked. Her face flushed and she looked suddenly like she was going to cry. Toxoplasmosis, transmitted through cat feces, causes brain and eye defects.

"I am a terrible mother," she said. "You told me to avoid cats." In nightmares she pictured the baby with stumps in place of his arms, convulsing uncontrollably.

"Kiddo's going to be okay, okay?" Dr. Murray said.

"Can't you give me a test?"

"We'll see about a test next time you're here. I have to get smarter about tests."

Then he asked where she would live after the baby was born. She said she was moving into her grandmother's house the following week. This seemed finally to settle a truce between them.

I left the room frustrated by the exchange. I couldn't understand why Amanda cared about her baby catching a rare disease when she poisoned her baby every day with carbon monoxide from cigarettes. In the free clinic, I'd met pregnant girls with similar histories whose previous children had been commandeered by the state and legal guardianship awarded to a distant relative. I did not often feel sympathy for these patients and I wondered if Amanda would face the same fate. I felt a zero-sum exchange had taken place, that even the good doctor could not plumb the depths of his experience and wisdom to convince Amanda of the real harms to her child. Dr. Murray, for his part, believed that just getting teenagers into the doctor's office every few weeks was a triumph. He believed also in the power of babies to reform parents. But he thought that healing happened over months and years, not in the twenty minutes of a clinic visit, and certainly not because of a grand speech from the doctor.

When the obstetrics rotation came to an end, I dropped my car at the Spokane airport and hitched a ride home with another medical student. The final exam was on a Tuesday morning in Seattle, and then I had four days for seeing my friends and family and catching up on sleep. On Saturday night I caught a puddle jumper back to Spokane. My plan was to crash with a classmate's parents in Spokane and early in the morning head out for Montana, turning south just before Butte, and arrive in Pocatello, Idaho, by dinnertime.

The flight from Seattle to Spokane was full and on time and I sat in the front row with a novel I'd picked up at the little bookstore I loved near my parents' house. I realized I had just a few more unencumbered hours. A day from now I would be immersed in pediatrics, and a thing as basic as reading fiction would fill me with guilt. I started into a story about a woman fleeing Cuba by boat. After we were airborne, the passenger sitting beside me asked if I was visiting Spokane. Generally I avoided conversation on airplanes, but she seemed so cheerful and unassuming that I said I was a medical student, had just spent six weeks in Spokane doing obstetrics, and was retrieving my car and moving on to southeast Idaho for another rotation.

She told me she had had recent experience with the medical field, then cleared her throat and said her husband had just died from non-Hodgkin's lymphoma. I turned my book over in my lap. Her face remained composed as she talked about going to his treatments on a strict schedule and how a sudden infection had come along and swept him away in one night. She said his treatment had been so costly that it had bankrupted them. He'd soldiered in pre-Vietnam campaigns, and her face turned flushed and teary as she described their failed fight to obtain health care through the Veterans Administration. They had run out of money entirely in the end and she hadn't been able to afford his funeral.

"What happened just this past Wednesday was that our church congregation donated ten thousand dollars to pay for the expenses," she said. "Can you believe that? I could hardly believe how generous people can be." I reached over and squeezed her hand, and her tears began to run. I glanced at the calendar resting on her thigh and saw she'd penciled in "platelets" for every other Wednesday at 9 A.M., which had to have been part of her husband's treatment. I shook my head and murmured sympathetically while she grew animated again. I felt how strongly she still wanted to fight and how she had just begun her grieving. I said I couldn't imagine how hard it was for her and her husband, and then sat back listening to her describe how a fellow vet had draped an American flag across his casket.

The flight came to a quick end, and when we bumped down on the runway she put on her cheerful public face again. We walked off the plane onto the foggy tarmac and she smiled breezily at me, then waved goodbye. I wondered what else I might have said to help her grieve and heal. I had seen and heard so many things from the extremes of life and I was still waiting for all those raw stories to add up to some kind of wisdom. Then I reclaimed my car and was on the road again, driving back through downtown Spokane. A warm feeling came through me as the familiar buildings passed by. I had worked hard and seen and felt so many things, and there was human frailty and suffering and strength everywhere around.

I was getting closer now.

CHAPTER 4

Pocatello

———⬥———

Baby Girl Mickelson arrived in the world thirteen weeks premature, after a crash cesarean section, and was immediately whisked to a surrogate womb in the neonatal intensive care unit, or NICU, where an around-the-clock nurse, intravenous medication, and respiratory support might keep her alive.

A pediatric resident named Jon was summoned to labor and delivery at 3 a.m. and ran into the operating room just as Baby Girl was being lifted out of her mother's abdomen, and now he related details of the resuscitation to the pediatric attending, Dr. Dave Gantry. Carrie and I, the brand new medical students in Pocatello, stood attentively trying to absorb Jon's fast presentation. Baby Girl's mother had started bleeding the previous afternoon, Jon said, and the trickling blood became bright, seeping stains within hours. Mom was breathless with crampy contractions when she walked through the emergency room door. While waiting for the doctor, she paced the emergency hallway restlessly, stopping to bend at the waist every seven minutes. She was in the twenty-seventh week of her pregnancy.

"Mom's ethanol level was 170," Jon continued automatically. The level was double the legal alcohol limit. "She had bruises on her abdomen and left arm." An ultrasound had predicted impending fetal demise and Baby Girl's heart rate plunged in a telling pattern of decelerations. The mother was strapped to a gurney and wheeled off to the operating suite with much hollering and kicking. She was a sturdy, petite Blackfoot Indian from the Fort Hall Reservation just north of Pocatello and she swung at the obstetrician as they went into the suite.

A corner of Jon's mouth twitched up in a half-smile and he said, "He ducked. She missed."

Jon had watery round eyes and his hair stood in a spiky crown about his head. He wore scrubs and a purple fanny pack stuffed full of tiny reference guides and examination tools, and when he turned in profile, the fanny pack looked like a battery for a human. He seemed to have irrepressible energy.

Now I marveled over Baby Girl, asleep in the incubator. She was small enough to rest comfortably in the palm of an adult hand and she appeared to float in a giant white plastic diaper. Her skin shone a bright ruddy hue. Jet-black hair hung in clumps against her temples and her eyes were shut. A tiny white tube burrowed down through one nostril and an IV line ran into her belly button, and her chest pumped up and down like a piston, breaths pulling the skin tightly between ribs. It was amazing that a human being could be so small and fragile.

Jon continued, "Baby came out in moderate respiratory distress with meconium everywhere. Lungs were suctioned extensively. Heart rate and pressures were fine. One- and five-minute Apgars were four and six. I got an umbilical line in. Overnight she was febrile to 39 degrees C and breathing 40 to 50 a minute on a 100 percent oxygen mask."

He said, "It looked twice like she might need intubation but she calmed with suctioning." Then he ran through arterial oxygen and carbon dioxide values and a list of laboratory results that sounded to me like a nonsensical jumble of numbers. As he talked I glanced around the NICU and noted that two infants were intubated. Thick plastic were hoses connected to their mouths and attached to mechanical ventilators, the machines huffing rhythmically. I wondered what problems they suffered and whether they would survive life support. Gradually I realized that all of the infants on the unit had tubes and lines running deep into their bodies like Baby Girl did. The incubators made the tiny patients seem like machines.

Dr. Gantry turned to face us. Carrie and I had arrived for that first day of the rotation wearing short white coats and skirts and we had the awkward, pressed look of new medical students.

"Why does she have a fever?" Gantry demanded. Gantry was six feet tall with the muscular bulk of a former football player. He wore a plaid shirt open at the collar with shirtsleeves rolled over his forearms and he carried himself with great confidence, as though he had achieved significant athletic success in his young adult life. He was a Texas transplant and the newest partner in a practice of eight pediatricians that looked after most local children and a couple thousand within a hundred-mile sweep of Pocatello.

I blinked a few times, swamped with details about the first seven hours of Baby Girl's life, and hesitantly said, "She could have an infection."

"What kind of infection?"

"Group B strep sepsis."

Gantry grinned. "You must have just done obstetrics."

"Yes."

"What else could she have?" He swooped down toward me. "Think like a pediatrician."

"Pneumonia. Meningitis."

"Good. Yes. Those are more common. I wonder if we know the results of Mom's strep cultures yet."

Jon perused his clipboard and said, "Her cultures were negative."

"So this isn't group B strep sepsis," Gantry mused. "But sepsis is still our best bet. Which organisms should you worry about?"

"*Listeria*," I said.

"*Haemophilus* and strep pneumo," Carrie added.

"Alright." Gantry looked off distantly, having gotten the lay of the land, and said, "Let's examine her."

Now Gantry opened the incubator windows and put a stethoscope to his ears. I reached into the humid, tropical incubator through a second window. When Baby Girl felt the pressure of our hands on her chest, her face wrinkled into a knot of features and her limbs began to jerk and tremble. A miniature hand reached for my stethoscope, fingers splayed. She clamped herself tightly onto the pinky finger I offered and wrestled me down vigorously. Through the stethoscope I heard rough breathing and her heart beating at a breakneck pace, with a loud mechanical heart murmur sounding through. I thought of how her heart must be no bigger than an adult fingernail, and I marveled at the sound of blood speeding through. Gantry pushed deeply on her soft belly. Suddenly a hard alarm began to sound and a nurse in starch-white tennis shoes hustled over and slapped the alarm off. Above the incubator I saw the infant's heart rate flashing red at 180 beats per minute. The nurse threaded her arm in through the window and rubbed Baby Girl's chest to calm her. After several moments the infant breathed normally again. The nurse raised an eyebrow at Gantry. He straightened and returned the look wordlessly.

Gantry turned again to me. "I want you to follow her from day to day," he said. This meant he expected me to take up Baby Girl's care under his supervision, as though I were the infant's primary doctor. "Jon will give you today's plan."

"You'll want to watch her respiratory status very carefully," Jon said briskly. "She got apneic a few times last night and may need to be intubated. You should follow that murmur and think about indomethacin if it persists. Her GI tract may not work yet, but we'll try tube feedings today. Her kidneys *are* working. Her bilirubin will climb, the question is how much. Pay attention to that. She's got blood cultures and a repeat chest x-ray pending. I started her on amp and gent last night. You can modify that when cultures come back."

I scribbled rapidly as plans continued to spill from Jon's mouth.

"Got all that?" Gantry said cheerfully.

I nodded, my head swimming with talk of organs, disease, and medications.

"Good. See her in the morning and present her on rounds," he said. Before I could reply, he had started for the next incubator.

Jon said, "So this is your first day."

I put on a determined smile and reminded myself that Jon was four years ahead in training, a second-year resident from the highly regarded Seattle Children's Hospital. Still, I couldn't imagine that midway through residency I would come off as knowledgeable and polished as he did. I suddenly felt afraid to show how little I knew after six months of clinical experience, and I was nagged by concern that I wouldn't perform well on the rotation. Above everything, I wanted to be inspired by pediatrics. I had cared for the occasional pediatric patient on previous rotations and been charmed by those who lived with disease, by bodies that healed with quick spontaneity, and I was eager for pediatrics to be my specialty of choice.

Then I looked at Baby Girl's chest heaving relentlessly and a jolt of terror passed through me. A human being's survival depended on what I elicited with my hands and stethoscope, on the numbers I shuffled around each morning, on treatment plans I concocted. The consequence of an oversight could be a worsened complication or even a patient's death.

"We'll go over the basics later today. You'll pick it up fast," Jon said.

I hadn't yet worked with a resident who had taken me in and coached and mentored me, and I said, "I'd appreciate that."

Every day of Baby Girl's first week of life, I discovered fresh signs of her deteriorating condition. Before morning rounds with Gantry, I sorted through nursing records and reports of the past day's events and examined her as gingerly and thoroughly as I could before triggering alarms and having my hand slapped by a vigilant NICU nurse. I learned to preempt the alarm by patting her chest softly, which often consumed precious minutes of pre-rounds. Then I'd sit down to determine my plan for the day before I met with Gantry, who had come to seem a bit of a bully. Rounds typically began with my rendition of Baby Girl's previous twenty-four hours, and then Gantry prodded me along with his specific and improbable questions.

At first we focused on Baby Girl's immature lungs, which were several weeks from breathing independently. She had gradually consumed higher and higher doses of oxygen, which indicated worsening stress on her lungs.

"She's receiving six liters of oxygen and required a mask overnight," I reported one morning later in the week. "They're suctioning up clear phlegm. Oxygen saturations were 92 to 93 percent on bi-pap."

Gantry leaned casually against an empty incubator, propped a hand on his waist, and began to talk and gesture as though convincing me to buy a car.

"First of all, she's got a developmental problem," he said.

"Right," I said, relieved to know the answer. "She can't make surfactant." I knew that no infant born at twenty-seven weeks gestation had the physiologic capability to produce surfactant, the protein that keeps lungs from collapsing. We were aerosolizing and spraying manufactured surfactant into her lungs until she could make the protein herself and I repeated this plan back to Gantry.

"Prematurity is clearly part of the oxygenation problem. Excellent," he said. I knew a more difficult question would follow the compliment. "You're addressing development issues and still she continues to get worse. What else might be causing lung problems and how do we figure that out?"

"We thought about pneumonia," I said.

"And the chest x-ray looks that way. What else could the x-ray suggest? You should be thinking of infant respiratory distress syndrome. IRDS." He pronounced the acronym as one word and talked about numeric parameters used to define IRDS.

I said, "She's also got a shunt."

"Yes," he agreed. "A patent ductus arteriosus. That will impair a baby's oxygenation." The ductus was a fetal remnant that shunted blood between the heart and the body, bypassing the lungs. In babies born at term, the shunt closed by day two of life as blood began to circulate through a pumping heart, and lungs learned to take up oxygen.

Now Gantry smiled like he had sold me the car. "Let me summarize. You're giving indomethacin and continuing her antibiotics. You've tried to determine why she's in respiratory distress, and meanwhile she's getting supportive care from your respiratory therapists."

As he broke Baby Girl's case into these small agreeable parts, I felt a rush of relief. Now the data were ordered and organized, we'd made contingency plans, and I felt that nothing had escaped our scrutiny. I exchanged a satisfied nod with Gantry.

He added airily, "Don't be surprised if she's intubated the next day or two."

"You think so?"

"She can't sustain this kind of respiratory effort. Believe me, she'll get tired from breathing so hard."

I looked away, wondering if something I had done had caused her lung failure. How did Gantry know she'd be intubated, and why hadn't I appreciated her slow swan dive toward machine ventilation? I realized I had confused my relief at having organized her clinical picture with relief that we had controlled her decline.

Gantry sensed my hesitation and said, "She's just not ready to breathe on her own yet. We've done the things we can do short of machine support."

I twisted my mouth around.

Gently Gantry said, "This is not unexpected."

As predicted, Baby Girl was intubated and put on a mechanical ventilator the next night, and still her woes continued unabated. She turned bright yellow. Her stomach rejected infant formula and she lost weight. At night Jon came across the hall at the apartment complex where WWAMI students and residents stayed to ask how she was faring. One night he sat at the kitchen table reviewing the complications of prematurity while I noted down everything he said. I was grateful for how earnestly he tried to teach his pediatric knowledge, and I memorized the notes while I stirred spaghetti sauce on the stove or relaxed on the sofa with a beer. When Baby Girl's belly bloated up a few days later, I knew to worry that her intestines were dying from oxygen deprivation. When her right arm and leg stopped moving, I wondered if an artery might have burst in her brain, and when I made these suggestions on our morning rounds, Gantry nodded agreeably. I began visiting Baby Girl two or three times each day—first thing in the morning and then on rounds with Gantry, and sometimes at lunch or right after clinic to track events that had happened during the day. My involvement became so intensive that I was thinking about medicine most waking moments and pediatrics finally seemed real. When I returned to the hospital after a weekend off, caring for patients came strangely and slowly to me until I insinuated myself back into the rhythm of the place.

Then a nurse was digging an elbow into my arm while I reviewed a day of Baby Girl's notes at the NICU counter. She whispered loudly, "Look who's come by."

A stout, petite woman walked shyly toward Baby Girl's incubator and instantly I knew who she was. Her hair was long and feathered at the sides and she wore a blue hospital robe over her gown. A girl of about five, wearing a lacy red dress and white tights, walked demurely at her side. The girl stood on tiptoe to see into the incubator and then looked at the woman, and they smiled an intimate, conspiratorial smile together. I noticed how starkly empty Baby Girl's incubator seemed compared with her neighbors' incubators, which were crowded with stuffed animals and pictures of siblings, parents, and grandparents.

The woman unlatched the incubator window and gently stroked Baby Girl's hair and arms. Baby Girl stretched languidly. *She knows,* I thought, *how does she know?* I turned away sharply. This was the first sighting I'd had of the woman in the ten days since Baby Girl's birth. Then I remembered what Jon had said the first morning about the mother's brisk bright bleeding and the crash C-section. I slipped off to the doctor's room with Baby Girl's thick chart and flipped to the first progress notes. The intake note described the mother as intoxicated and belligerent in the emergency room. A blood alcohol level twice the legal limit was circled and underlined and a note from the obstetrician recounted how the mother had swung at him. He added parenthetically that he believed domestic abuse had triggered her uterine hemorrhage. I snapped the chart closed and returned angrily to the NICU. I wanted to probe the mother about the story, to see if I could separate speculation from reality, but the woman and her daughter had disappeared.

Occasionally during the next few weeks I saw the father hovering briefly by the incubator. He wore tight black jeans and a shiny Steelers football jacket and he kept his hands in his pockets. The nurses eyed him from a distance. He pretended not to see their pointed looks, asked no questions, and neither Gantry nor I ever chanced to speak with him about the infant's condition. After his short visits he lingered in the hallway for a few minutes and then vanished. Inside, I burned to ask him if he felt remorse or responsibility for a daughter who lived in a cage, who needed machines to make her human.

Later I asked Gantry if the state should get involved.

He weighed the question for several moments before he said finally, "I know that's an issue." He paused heavily again and said, "Unfortunately, Mom never pressed charges and he doesn't have a record." I felt something in him slump back. He talked of the state's approach to child abuse in Native American families, where questions of castigation and remedy fell to the tribe. He spoke coolly, as though he had justified the policy innumerable times to himself and to patients at risk and had finally, unwillingly, submitted to the reality of the situation.

Then Baby Girl's health turned dramatically better in a matter of three days and she took formula and gained weight, her lungs breathed freely, and she graduated to using just a sniff of oxygen blown at her nose. Her heart murmur disappeared altogether. When I visited in the mornings she opened her eyes and blinked anxiously, looked around the incubator, and distracted herself with my fingers. One afternoon when I wandered through the NICU I spotted a nurse feeding her bottle formula, and we grinned at each other. Baby Girl wore a yellow and white stocking cap and looked like a regular newborn.

Finally Baby Girl's family found her on their radar screen and named her Allison Rae. This event jolted me out of the cocoon I'd spun for myself, where fragile babies were snatched back from the edge of death and lived on happily. I knew little about the world she would inherit and thought of her discharge home anxiously.

I would often be reminded of how much that outside world mattered.

In my email one evening was a message from Seattle asking to trade a rotation later that winter: Seattle internal medicine for internal medicine in Missoula, Montana. I leaned forward in my chair and scrolled through the message. An Alaska student was tired of being in WWAMI-land, away from her Seattle husband, and hoped to come back to Seattle. The coordinator who had sent the email also dangled an open spot at the veterans hospital in Boise, Idaho, where medical students worked on teams with medicine residents and attending physicians, and local vets gave the place WWAMI flavor. She reiterated that medical students had given Boise the highest marks of any site in internal medicine.

I leaned back, closed my eyes, and rubbed my tired face. I reviewed how my car had sledded into a soft snowbank that morning, the steering wheel suddenly disconnected from reality when I'd backed out of the driveway. Overnight eight inches of new snow had fallen in Pocatello, the temperature rode steady in the twenties, and all day conversation in the clinic was about shoring up for winter. I thought of how a city worker had just happened along the lane, hopped out of his pickup, and said, "I guess you better get back in your car." He'd attached a chain to the bottom of my trunk and popped the car back on the road in five minutes. I imagined a whole winter of freezing air and icy roads and Seattle news and gossip transmitted by email.

I had to be the only medical student who was seriously considering the swap.

After dinner I cleared the table and sat down with my journal and wrote about how much I loved rural medicine and how WWAMI doctors were the real thing. I closed the notebook having failed to muster a fair argument for the other side, understood what my gut feeling was, and knew my mind was made up.

The next afternoon I called from the hallway phone in back of the pediatrics clinic and asked if I could go to Missoula later that winter.

A four-year-old named Anne Salisbury was sitting on the table when I came in the exam room. She was kicking her legs together and making choo-choo sounds. Her mother sat in the corner, reading out loud about a talking caboose. Anne pointed at me when I came in and said, "Are you the doctor?" Her voice was high and musical.

Her mother smiled, put the book down, and stood to shake my hand. I introduced myself.

"The little caboose is our favorite story, right Annie?" Mom said. "Let's finish reading after we visit with the doctor."

"Okay," Anne said, her head bobbing.

I turned to Mom and said, "What brings you in today?"

"I have an ear infection!" Anne said.

To Anne I said, "Which ear bothers you?"

Anne pointed first at her left ear and then at her right ear.

"She's been pulling on that right ear a couple days," Mom said. "She's had a lot of ear infections. It's all in the chart. But we've been good, just one this year." I asked about fevers and cough and changes in her appetite, and Mom answered while Anne swiveled back and forth on the exam table.

"Let's look at your ears," I said, standing.

Anne clapped her hands over her ears as I reached for the otoscope and fitted a new plastic cone over the strong light.

"Annie, tell her who's hiding in your ears."

I put one hand on a hip and said, "Is Bugs Bunny hiding in your ear?"

Anne made a face and pulled back.

"No," she said.

"Why don't I take a look," I said. I pushed back her hair and zoomed in on her left ear with the scope. To my relief, she sat patiently.

"You sure that's not Bugs Bunny?"

"It's Barney!" she said indignantly.

"Right," I said. "Now I see him."

"I thought Barney was in the other ear," Mom said. She winked at me.

Anne pointed at her right ear. "Baby Bop is in this ear!"

I glanced over at Mom and she nodded.

I moved around to Anne's other side and saw that her eardrum was red, and the membrane remained fixed when I blew a puff of air into her ear.

Anne drew back the moment she felt the air on the drum and frowned and I stood back for a moment.

"Did you see Baby Bop?" Mom said.

"Not sure I did. Maybe I should check again."

Anne nodded solemnly. I bent to visualize the inflamed eardrum again.

"There's Baby Bop!"

"I thought so," Anne said.

That night I walked across the hall at the apartment complex and knocked on Jon's door, looking for some advice. He was playing the guitar inside and I heard him stop midsong and come to the door.

"What's up?" he said, leaning against the doorframe. He was still in scrubs.

"The Bugs Bunny thing didn't work today."

"No?" he said sympathetically.

"And who is this Baby Bop?"

"Ah, yes, Baby Bop. She's Barney's little sidekick." He made his voice high and squeaky and said, "She talks like this."

"And when did this Baby Bop become the thing?"

"It's very new," Jon said. "You've got to keep up with these things."

He won't eat nothing. He refuses," Angel said. She was an eighteen-year-old making her first pass at motherhood, and she sat cross-legged in a chair, rocking her body with arms tightly crossed. She seemed sleep-deprived and her voice was thin. She threw a critical look at the infant, Jacob, who lay bundled and still in a yellow blanket on the examining table a few feet from her. Then she looked at Dr. Gantry. Her pale creamy face was heavy with eye makeup.

Dr. Gantry turned to Carrie and me. "This poor lady has been taking care of a very sick child," he said. He said that a rare condition called Werdnig-Hoffman disease had caused Jacob's muscles to begin disintegrating at birth. I studied the baby for a moment. He was bundled and hadn't moved yet but gave no sign of having a disease, although his cheeks seemed flat. Later, Gantry would tell us that patients with Werdnig-Hoffman typically grew weaker and weaker over several months and died before their first birthday. The last few days of his life, he'd lie still, gasping flaccidly for breath.

Now Jacob opened his eyes with a slight movement and suddenly there was nothing in the room except his face. We all honed in on his right eye, which was coated with a bright bloody film. Gantry gently straightened the baby on the table, watching intently and clucking his tongue.

"He's not focusing on anything," Gantry said. Carrie and I pressed against the table. After a moment I saw Jacob's eyes moving independently of each other, one eye gazing left while the second veered down to his feet, his eyes moving like pool balls sliding haphazardly across a table.

"How long has this been going on? With the eyes?" Gantry demanded. He suddenly seemed enormous in the room.

Angel paused. "I never noticed that."

"The red eye?"

"Oh," she said. "The red eye was last week." She took a long look at Jacob.

"Did you worry about that eye?"

"Yes."

"Did you think about bringing him in?"

"He seemed okay," she said crossly.

Gantry unwound the infant's blanket with great care, as though he thought Jacob might spill out in a pile of crumbs. He cradled the infant's head and neck in his wide, thick palm and lifted the body away from the jumper. Then he placed Jacob on the exam table, the thin shiny paper crackling once underneath. The room became deathly quiet as the infant remained motionless on the table. I saw that his legs had lost baby fat and his skin hung loose off the muscle. His lips were calm and dry and he made no attempt to cry. I moved his arms first, then his legs, and when I let go the limbs flopped down heavily on the table.

"Is this Werdnig-Hoffman?" I asked. It didn't seem that the rare disease accounted for all of the infant's problems.

"This is partly Werdnig-Hoffman," Gantry said.

"What's wrong with my baby?" Angel said plaintively.

"We call this 'failure to thrive,'" he said coolly. "We're going to step out and look at x-rays now. We'll be back."

In the radiology suite he shuffled through a stack of manila envelopes and said, "What are you trying to pick up on the x-rays?"

I was still stuck on the neuromuscular explanation and said I didn't know if we would find anything.

Fump fump fump. Gantry put x-rays on the light board with a flick of the wrist and we leaned in toward the images. I felt a disbelieving protest rise and tickle my throat.

"Oh my God," Carrie said, hand covering mouth.

"This is the skeletal survey," Gantry said grimly. "A skull film, a chest film, extremity films."

We stood numb and silent considering the breaks and spaces that interfered with the pristine lines of a left femur, a right tibia. A bright white spot just above the ankle indicated the healed bone of an old injury. With his index finger Gantry tapped on four fractures along the smooth curves of ribs. After a moment he took down these films and held up skull films, curving and bending in his hand. *Fump fump fump.* Immediately I saw that Jacob's skull buckled inward just above his right eye. In a moment cross-sectional views of Jacob's brain were on the board and Carrie pointed to a bright blood clot that lit up in back of his head. The ordinary curls and tufts of brain tissue had been pushed aside by clot, and normally clean symmetric lines were skewed and aslant. Later we would learn to call the fractures "nonaccidental trauma."

"How the hell can that be?" Angel said, standing indignantly when Gantry brought the news.

Gantry's football player form filled the doorway. "You'll be best able to answer that question," he replied curtly. Angel looked stunned.

"I don't know *nothing* about this," she said.

"We're going to put Jacob in intensive care," Gantry said. He turned and herded Carrie and me to the back corner of the emergency department. Carrie was still shaking her head.

"Carrie, I want you to follow this patient," he said.

Several hours after Jacob moved to intensive care, he suffered a thrashing, full-body seizure. He seized again while we were on rounds in the pediatric intensive care unit, or PICU, the next morning and I saw his legs contract and arms fly through the air as if freed from gravity. His spooky blind eyes rolled mercilessly, untethered from anything inside him. The sound of his limbs pounding the mattress was hollow and rhythmic and if I turned away, I could imagine the noise to be that of a temperamental child.

The following evening at the apartment, Carrie reported on Angel's insistence on ignorance. "I know it doesn't make sense, but I believe her," Carrie said. Angel's boyfriend had been taken to the police station for questioning and like Angel had issued bland denials. He came and went from the house and wasn't always around, he said. When Jacob's eye had turned red, he had coaxed Angel to bring the infant to the doctor.

Angel's boyfriend came through the PICU several days later. Carrie and I watched him waltz into Jacob's room, acting as though he hadn't seen us sitting at the nursing desk. He was twenty-four with long dark hair falling down his back and a face scarred by acne. He slid behind Angel, steered her out into the hall, and began to speak roughly to her. "Are you going to talk to me, baby? Are you going to tell me what's going on or are you going to blow me off like usual?" I could see Angel's face cast toward the floor, unable to meet his blazing eyes. Carrie and I looked at each other in horror. A nurse reached for the phone.

"Unbelievable," Carrie whispered.

He went to jail a day later. What we heard was that he'd admitted to shaking Jacob to quiet him down. Later, Angel told Carrie she'd believed for a long time that something was wrong but couldn't blame anybody except herself. The boyfriend had babysat while she ran an errand the previous week, and the infant's lethargy and bloody eye had come on gradually in the following days. She couldn't turn the boyfriend in because she hadn't known for sure.

"What could I have said?" she wailed.

Later when she saw films of cracked ribs and bone dangling from bone she began to shake violently, then leaned over covering her face with her hands for a long time.

The night that Jacob lapsed into a protracted seizure and died of suffocation, neither Carrie nor I were on call. We heard the news just before morning rounds and sat in agonized silence as the post-call attending doctor presented two cases seen overnight and reported on Jacob's resuscitation and death. When our turn to discuss hospital patients came, we went one after another and fumbled, forgot, skipped over pertinent information. Afterward, Gantry complained with great vitriol about everything we had missed in our presentations. I nodded pertly and promised to work on it. Carrie's face clouded over blankly. She seemed consumed with grief and outrage over Jacob's demise, and I felt her powerlessness deeply. We moved numbly through morning rounds and then walked down the hill to the clinic. Carrie unwound her scarf slowly, dropped her gloves on a chair, and straightened her immaculate white coat. We hadn't talked much all morning.

The moment we came out of the back office, nurses thrust charts at us and pointed us cheerfully toward the exam rooms.

Hello, darling," Jon screeched from the door, a dead ringer for Daffy Duck.

He came in the apartment with his guitar and played fitfully while Carrie and I studied at the kitchen table. When he put the guitar down we talked about congenital heart defects, and he quizzed us on the sounds of murmurs that Gantry would lecture on later that week. I had already seen several children with heart defects at the hospital and now memorized the disorders smoothly. Then the conversation slipped into residency talk and my ears pricked up. Jon said he'd banked on the Pocatello experience to reassure himself that he loved the daily practice of pediatrics and reaffirm that he wanted to be a doctor. He had muddled through seventeen months of sleeplessness at the insular mothership of Seattle Children's Hospital and arrived at the midpoint of his residency, and Pocatello hadn't immediately recharged him the way he'd hoped. I listened intently, knowing that Jon represented a vision of what my life would be like in three or four years.

"One of these days I might kill a patient," Jon said. He said he didn't often read about medicine when he was away from the hospital. He wanted to preserve those rare hours for music and flying and being with friends. One hundred hours of patient care every week numbed him intellectually. He had loved biochemistry and physiology in medical school, but the imprecision of clinical medicine had been a disappointment, and he felt he wasn't a good doctor because his attention wasn't fully on medicine.

I said I disagreed. I had worked with him one afternoon in the clinic and loved his bedside manner. He was gentle and calming with infants, and his cartoon voices drew smiles and laughs from scared children. He listened thoughtfully to the moms, considered their needs, attended to issues that weren't medical. He clearly cared about the quality of his doctoring, and he was sharp with medicine.

I wondered if patients like Baby Girl or Jacob might have muddled his appreciation of clinical science.

"It's not the hundred-hour weeks," he said. I knew many residents didn't like to admit they weakened under stress or fatigue and I guessed that this applied to Jon too. Still, after he went across the hall for the night I sat on the couch worrying over whether he'd give up medicine, and I wondered if I'd have the stamina to get through a grueling residency like his.

What I understood was how badly he wanted to be gone from the hospital. Many evenings he'd drive to the airfield near Chubbuck, a few miles out of town in the shadow of the local phosphate plant. He'd climb into a Cessna 172, slide the cushiony black headphones over his ears, and lift off into the great wide space, piercing the dark starry sky in his humming aircraft. He'd be lost into that beautiful automatic world for a time and when he came back he was okay again.

I believe he returned when he no longer felt the sting and strain of the hospital, when his questions subsided for a time and everything internal seemed orderly again.

Stories continued to arrive at the clinic in family packages. Fiona, the mother, rocked one-year-old Hester in her lap. The father, Jack, stood by the exam table. A preschool-age boy with wide green eyes played on the floor. They were from a town named Grace, an hour from Pocatello.

When we walked into the exam room, Fiona bent around Hester to get her face deliberately close to the boy and shouted, "Knock it off, Grant. Sit still." Grant had been pushing a toy car in a wide arc across the floor and for a moment he stopped. Then avoiding the looks of both his parents he resumed softly revving the car's engine. Jack frowned and put his foot over the car as Grant drove past his corner. The room stunk of stale smoke.

Fiona straightened herself and swung Hester's legs around so they both faced the pediatrician, Dr. Paula Best. I worked infrequently with Best, who practiced half-time at the office in order to have more than just evenings at home with her two small children. A few years back, her pregnancies had put the practice in a twist, since her absence meant months of extra hospital work and night calls for everyone else. Whatever rifts had been associated with the pregnancies seemed to have blown over. The few times I'd worked with her I had been a little awestruck by the ease with which she floated through the clinic. She was always beautifully groomed and her voice was rich and deep and authoritative. She seemed used to having things her way. At work she presented a glamorous confidence, and patients and families responded warmly to her.

Now Dr. Best handed me Hester's chart and suggested I scan her medical history.

Fiona looked at me and snapped, "Her cold's no better. You'll see it in there. It's been three months she's had this runny nose. We're pretty sick of it." This sprung out as a small explosion. Fiona's face was angular with wide-set dark brown eyes.

Best crossed her legs. "First things first. Did you quit smoking?" she asked.

"We tried that."

The doctor's eyebrow twitched and then settled. "How long did you quit?"

"We quit an entire two weeks and it didn't work," Fiona said.

Jack cleared his throat and spoke through closed teeth. "We smoke outside," he said. A droopy mustache gave his face the look of perpetual sadness.

"No," Best said. A cold assertiveness came over her. "Smoke travels through cracks and gets on clothes. You have to realize how irritating smoke is for infant lungs." She clicked perfect pink fingernails on the desk.

"Look, we tried it and it didn't work," Fiona said, narrowing her eyes. "We need to get this problem fixed today and we're not leaving until you come up with something new."

"She just ain't better," Jack said. He shuffled his feet and pushed knotted fists farther into his jacket pockets.

As I unfolded Hester's chart I considered what solution might satisfy the family—perhaps a miracle drug to dry up Hester's runny nose or a high-tech machine to purify the trailer air. I flipped to the most recent progress notes and read about ear infections and an asthma attack severe enough that Fiona had rushed Hester to the emergency room. At six months of age Hester had come down with a ravaging case of croup and was admitted to the hospital for several days for treatment. Sometimes her fevers ran as high as 104 degrees.

When I turned the page I saw an entry about Jack being laid off work and the family living on thin savings. Now I wondered how they had stretched to pay for doctor visits, a hospital stay, medications, and I thought of how patients whose families didn't pay the bills had their charts taped shut. Even gasoline for the drive from Grace wasn't a trivial expense. I continued through the chart, trying to affect a casual face about what I read next. At a recent visit, Best had checked Hester for bruises and ordered a torso x-ray. My disbelief lasted about three seconds. Coolly, I studied Jack. Now I thought that his body language suggested a coiled violence, and I had felt resentment and anger in his voice. I thought he was as capable of abuse as Baby Girl's father or Angel's boyfriend. Fiona presented herself as no poor, weak waif either, having gone on the offensive the moment we'd walked in the room. Fragile little Hester was the center of attention in that uncompromising world and this made her as vulnerable as anyone.

Fiona and Best were sparring back and forth over remedies when I heard Fiona say, "We ain't doing food stamps. We can borrow. We'll pay back when we can."

The tone in the room changed. Jack gave a subtle nod in the corner. Best squeezed her lips together, blinked her long eyelashes, and conceded. I looked up from the chart, feeling unexpected sympathy for Fiona and her world filled with a wriggly son, a husband out of work, dwindling savings, a chronically sick infant.

"Alright, let's take another look at Hester," Best said, reaching for the baby.

She looked hastily into Hester's ears and then unsnapped her jumper buttons in one swift movement. As we listened to the throaty rattle in Hester's chest I could not help noticing the pearly smoothness of her baby skin. Best sat down at her desk and began to write a laundry list of asthma triggers for Fiona and Jack to check for at home. I turned back to the chart, scanning through notes for any signs of trauma, and didn't know if I was surprised or not by the answer in the notes. A month earlier, Best had documented that she'd seen no bruises on two separate occasions. An x-ray had come up pristine and fractureless.

Then I felt remorse sweep through me. How rapidly I had passed judgment and willingly trusted a stereotype. That mistrust might save one infant's life but would be a disservice to every other struggling family. Now I wondered if similar suspicions about abuse had caused the original delay in getting Hester's asthma under control. I thought about how the visit had become doctor versus patient, and I leaned against the wall thinking of how I'd put aside the idea of relating to my patients. I chastened myself to think about what we could do for Fiona and Jack in the remaining few minutes of the visit and considered how I could offer an inkling of sympathy and appreciation for their difficult lives.

Finally I saw the rocky life in a town called Grace, a hard-working mother, an unemployed father, two busy children growing up in that limited place. Hester's asthma would come on intermittently with no permanent remedy except the hope that she might outgrow the condition as a teenager. I did not like that Fiona and Jack continued to smoke, but I knew that shouldn't stop us from wanting to help them. Hester's disease was locked in with the immutable conditions of their lives.

Best turned from the desk and handed Fiona the list she'd written along with prescriptions for antibiotics and a deconges-tant. She was all gloss again, unruffled, and bringing the visit to a quick end. I wondered what swirled beneath that cheer-ful veneer and settled upon some combination of irritation, empathy, and the heaviness of knowing she could not alter the overarching reality of lives. Fiona stood. Jack bent down and scooped up Grant, and we followed them out the door.

After Thanksgiving, a seasoned pediatrician named Betty Charles took up the inpatient service, giving Dr. Gantry a respite. One afternoon while we ate lunch in the hospital cafeteria, she flipped through a catalog of all-terrain vehicles featuring leather-clad bikers cresting dirt mounds and leaning low into turns. I smiled listening to her describe the dirt bike she hoped to buy for her son's sixteenth birthday. While she talked she arranged her stained dishes and utensils in a tall pile on her tray. Her hands were tanned and creased. Then she leaned in and said solemnly, "You drink bottled water?"

I shook my head.

Lowering her voice, Charles said that a few years back, when they'd lived in Pocatello, their newborn calves had arrived in the world with egregious birth defects. She and her husband owned a working ranch, she said. Several of the calves born in Pocatello had come out with just two or three legs.

It intrigued me that Charles supplemented pediatrics with a small cattle operation, and I guessed that she ranched out of some leathery family predisposition rather than for financial reasons.

"It's got to be the hydrocarbons," she said. "They've leaked into the water table for decades."

I had nothing to contribute to the conversation, and I continued to chew my sandwich and chips.

"Soon as we moved outside of Pocatello city limits, we never had problems with the calves again. Good calves for eight years. You think that's a coincidence?"

"Sounds like a pattern," I said agreeably.

"What I'm getting at is why all those kids upstairs have holes in their hearts," she said.

I put down my sandwich and took a swallow of water.

"Hydrocarbons?" I said. Now I thought about the fertilizer plant along Interstate 84 at the fringes of Pocatello, the edifice of steel pipes and towers woven up with orange sodium lights, and twenty-story columns belching great steamy clouds like a giant downed spaceship. I knew the plant employed hundreds of people in southeast Idaho, but I suffered a visceral reaction every time I drove past and had almost been hoping to blame human disease on factory discharges.

"Have you noticed how much congenital heart disease there is at the hospital?" Charles said.

"It seems like a lot." But I hadn't seen pediatrics anywhere besides Pocatello, so I had nothing to compare.

I thought of the month-old infant we had hospitalized, one who desperately needed surgery to repair a defect between her left and right ventricles. In one month's time I'd met more than a few babies who'd arrived in the world with leaks and holes between chambers of the heart, their blood vessels wrongly attached in acts of inattentive plumbing, organs stunted by some unknowable prenatal spell. Two had been in and out of the hospital the whole month. Walking past their rooms on the pediatric floor, I heard oxygen hissing through masks and saw cool mist hovering above the infants blue and puffy with fluid.

When the tiny hearts dilated and clogged up with fluid, the only recourse was major surgery.

Andrea Snowe was a shy high school freshman with curly gold hair, bright blue eyes, and a failing heart. She'd been born with a pulmonary valve several sizes too small, a misplaced aorta, and a gaping hole between the ventricles that shunted blood into a futile, oxygen-deprived cycle. By two months of life, blue and stunted, she lay on the operating table undergoing an eleven-hour surgery to repair her failing heart, and the surgery came out successfully. Dr. Best, who had known Andrea since kindergarten, told me Andrea had enjoyed a normal childhood and grown on pace with her peers. But the previous summer a certain fatigue had crept into her, limiting her stamina to dance, and an ultrasound of her heart had showed surgical repairs beginning to disintegrate. In the last few weeks her heart function had slowed to two-thirds capacity and her heart had dilated and filled with fluid.

"This will gradually progress until she's breathless just sitting on the couch," Best said.

Best smoothed her shirtsleeves and told me that mother and daughter had just returned from a visit to Salt Lake City, where Andrea had undergone extensive evaluation of her heart. White-coated technicians had sucked countless tubes of blood from her arms and graded her exercise stamina with treadmills and breathing machines, and she'd filled out stacks of health questionnaires. After much deliberation among cardiologists, she was finally entered onto the bottom of the transplant waiting list.

"Andrea's mother wants us to put a positive spin on things," Best said. "She wants Andrea to live a normal teenage life, and I think that's a reasonable goal. But Andrea's probably got a year before her heart gives in and I think she knows this even though I've never hinted as much. She's a smart kid. She knows what's happening to her body." Best instructed me to check Andrea's feet. Whenever her feet and ankles were swollen with fluid, she wore her soft dance sneakers. The swollen feet meant her heart was overloaded with excess fluid and she was in heart failure.

Now Best glided into the room ahead of me. Andrea was

sitting on her hands and looked shyly at the floor. Mom sat close beside her, an arm wrapped around the teenager's hunched back. Andrea wore a Mickey Mouse sweatshirt and, I noticed immediately, shimmery silver flats. Her feet were barely swollen.

"How are you, Andrea?" Best asked, dropping onto her chair. It was late in the afternoon and Andrea had just been let off class for the day.

"I'm okay."

"How was school today?"

Andrea sheepishly shook her head of beautiful flaxen curls. "Fine," she said.

After a moment, Mom said, "She quit the dance team."

"Now, what's that about?" Best leaned down and tried to meet her eyes.

"I feel *way* too tired by the end of school," Andrea said. Later Mom told us confidentially that Andrea hated the way her swollen legs looked in her dance uniform.

"How is school?"

"Alright."

"Not great?"

Andrea shook her head. Mom said, "She's missed three or four days since we got back from Salt Lake, and I just can't get her to school because I leave so early for work."

"So you're missing quite a bit," Best said, making a note on the chart. She tilted her head and studied the quiet teenager with a look of concern. Andrea pushed her lips together. Then Best reached into her pocket for her stethoscope and we listened to Andrea's heart beating steadily, a murmur lingering between heart sounds.

Finally Best straightened up and said, "You're on the transplant list. That's good news."

Andrea looked up. "But it could take forever," she said. "Like years."

"Andrea!"

Best said, "You are right that transplants depend upon some things out of our control. But the process is moving in the right direction. You're listed now, and we've learned that your blood type is favorable, which means a shorter wait. After transplant, I expect you'll live a normal life. And in the meantime, I think it's a good idea to live as normal a life as you can."

Andrea sighed. I wasn't so far off in age that I romanticized adolescence and I guessed that Andrea felt that no one understood her body or the emotional swings of her heart condition.

"Do you want to try medicine to improve your energy level? I think it would be a good idea."

Now Andrea and Mom both nodded vigorously. Best looked meaningfully at me and wrote out a prescription for fluoxetine, the generic form of Prozac.

"This takes four to six weeks to work, so don't give up because you still feel kind of slow next week," Best said. "Anyway, come back and visit me in ten days. Let's see how you feel then. Make an appointment when you walk out."

Afterwards, Best dictated her report into a hand-held tape recorder, combing a hand through her hair and speaking briskly in the machine. For the plan she said, "Return in ten days, sooner if worsening breathing or fatigue." She clicked off the recorder and paused before dropping it onto a stack of charts atop her desk. She said to no one in particular, "Ten days is probably overcautious." I could sense her attachment to Andrea and knew she didn't want to lose her patient. I had heard doctors say from time to time that they "treated themselves" as well as the patient and now I understood how such a thing could be true.

M adison was a three-month-old infant who lay cheerfully on the exam table while Dave Gantry snapped his fingers in an arc above her. The baby flashed a cheeky smile and reached for Gantry while he bantered with Mom and Dad about Idaho State basketball. Now Madison arched her back, stretched for Gantry's snapping fingers, and her expression turned anxious. Suddenly a hint of purple appeared under her translucent skin and spread up from her toes and fingertips. A breathless cry bubbled from her blue lips and her face turned ashy as Mom scooped her off the table, murmuring and bouncing her gently. She turned to Gantry and apologized while she rocked the baby, and I saw that baby and Mom shared the same round hazel eyes and broad cheeks. Gantry leaned down and clucked close to Madison's ear.

"That's what happens," Mom said.

"And it's getting worse," Dad said. He was cleanly shaved and looked about thirty years old. His feet were planted in unlaced high-top sneakers.

Finally a pink flush came to Madison's face and Gantry said, "That was a pretty good spell." He turned to me with his eyebrows raised and said, "You won't forget that."

As an afterthought, he said, "What does she have?"

"Some kind of cyanotic heart disease," I said.

He said, "Tetrology of Fallot."

"She's not eating very well anymore. She gets real tired when she eats," Dad said.

Gantry and I put stethoscopes to Madison's chest while Mom held her. Sounds wrapped around every heartbeat and the heartbeat itself went like a snare drum. When I looked up, Madison's face was filled with worry. I had never seen a look of worry on an infant's face before.

Gantry said kindly, "She's got to come down to Salt Lake for surgery." I hung my stethoscope around my neck and crossed my arms. I was impressed by how swiftly he'd made this major decision.

Dad turned pale and said, "We wondered if that time had come."

"How long is the surgery?" Mom asked.

"Could take ten hours, maybe more," Gantry said.

"And then what happens?"

"And then, if everything goes well, she's a normal baby again. She eats normally, she grows to a normal height and weight. She goes off to school. The repairs will last fifteen to twenty years, sometimes longer."

"I guess we head on down there, then," Dad said.

After the daylong cardiology clinic at the health department, which was housed in a standard two-story government building circa 1970 on Frontage Road in Pocatello, I gathered my backpack and winter parka and walked out, passing a door labeled "Maternal and Child Health" in the twisting corridor. I stopped at the end of the hallway and turned back and went through the Maternal and Child Health door. A clerk looked up from her desk.

I explained who I was and asked if the health department collected statistics on congenital heart disease in the region.

"Let me check," she said. She went to a tan-colored metal file cabinet behind the desk, brought out a spiral-bound booklet, and flipped through. "We count the number of cases of heart disease," she said. "Is that what you need?"

"I'm curious if the incidence is higher in southeast Idaho than in other parts of the country," I said.

She shook her head slowly. "We don't do anything like that. Do you want to see this?" She handed me the booklet.

The page she had opened to showed data that was two years old. There had been two cases of bulbis cordis anomaly, seven cases called "other congenital anomalies of heart," and two cases of circulatory anomaly. Eleven cases in all. No other information had been collected.

Between patients one afternoon I cornered Gantry, who I'd come to respect deeply as a doctor and teacher, and I asked him about Pocatello's level of congenital heart disease.

"You always hear people say the rate is higher here," he said. He mulled over the thought and added, "The rate probably is higher, because of random chance." I nodded. I had read about small towns with excessive cases of lymphoma or neurologic disease and understood that some towns had higher-than-average rates of certain diseases and some lower-than-average rates, and the discrepancy rested with statistical probability; very rarely is there real cause and effect between pollutants and disease. Even so, it was tempting to blame the excess disease on something tangible, like Pocatello's phosphate processing plant that had recently been declared a Superfund cleanup site.

"What about hydrocarbons?" I said.

"No," he said. "Not to say that never happens, but I don't think that's the case here."

He shook his head contemplatively, and said the hardest thing to learn was that a child could fall deathly ill out of plain old bad luck.

I returned to Seattle at Christmastime and met Jon at a popular sushi restaurant on Forty-fifth Street several weeks later. We squeezed into a corner table, where I could hear the pouring rain just outside the foggy restaurant windows. Several people were crammed in the entryway waiting to sit.

Jon held up a laminated menu and scanned the fish list. "I missed this," he said, grinning. He looked wan and thin after having been on call on the busy toddler service every third night, and I felt odd seeing him in the familiar restaurant that was part of my Seattle life, far from wwami-land.

"But I miss Pocatello," I said. We ordered eel and spicy tuna and yellowtail and sipped green tea. I told him I was convinced that I wanted to be a pediatrician, maybe even in a rural place. I had been contemplating the residency program at Seattle Children's. If I could be anything like the doctor that Jon had become, I said, I would be very pleased. Jon said he thought I would do well wherever I chose to go. He asked about the rotation I had just begun in internal medicine. I had been assigned to the Veterans Hospital in Seattle for the first of three months, and I shrugged.

"It's good but not quite the same," I said. I was back in the hospital one hundred hours per week and had already started bonding with the medicine residents on my team. The grind felt different than Pocatello, though, where I had been so close to patients' lives.

I asked about the toddler service and Jon's voice dropped to a soft pitch. He said he just didn't think he was cut out for medicine. He had thought a lot over the holidays and had made an appointment with his residency director to discuss dropping out. The expression on his face was severe.

"What will you do?"

A smile passed across his mouth. "I'll fly more," he said, and for a moment he seemed elsewhere. He had memorized the requirements for a commercial aviation license and was thinking of becoming a pilot. It would take years—as long as it had taken to get to this stage in his medical training.

"Is that the right thing to do?" I said. I thought he was a wonderful doctor but I also thought he should be happy. "Maybe it will be different when you're out practicing, you know, when you're done with residency."

He was still smiling, and I felt heartened. His struggle made residency training seem less of a fortress and more of a process, and I was glad for my future sanity that he could wrestle with his reasons for being in medicine and still be considered a serious physician.

After dinner we hugged goodbye and I did not see him for months, when we passed on the run in the cafeteria at Children's Hospital. He hadn't dropped out of residency and his weariness seemed to have eased somewhat. I felt a surge of gratitude again for how much he'd contributed towards my clinical skills and for the glimpse he'd given me into a young physician's soul.

We had been through a chapter together.

CHAPTER 5

Missoula

Missoula existed as a kind of fable in my mind. I had known the place briefly, from stories told in bars between dart games and pitchers of beer, from excursions into steep western Montana forests and Norman Maclean stories filtered through slack moments at night before my plunge into sleep. I nourished dreams of luminous mountains, thrashing summer storms, chanterelles growing in the cool damp shade of fallen timber.

Patients' lives bled into my daydreaming. People arrived in Seattle from Montana towns named Ajax and Deer Lodge and Wolf Creek, half-alive and propelled by an almost unbearable instinct to keep going. For a month I took care of a middle-aged man named Billy Wayne Packer who was crushed between an eighteen-wheeler and his own pickup truck while he was patching a flat tire. Somehow he extricated himself from between the vehicles, crawled into the cab of his pickup truck, and drove fifteen miles down a dirt road to the hospital in Livinston.

"I was so thirsty. Really, really thirsty. I just had to keep going, because I knew I was going to die," he said.

He forgot everything after the hazy bumpy drive. The chart notes from Livingston report he bled rapidly into his gut, his blood pressure low and skittery. A surgeon in Bozeman opened his belly, carved out the hemorrhaging pieces, shipped the living remnants of him by helicopter airlift to Seattle in the middle of the night. Packer awoke in intensive care with just four feet of digestive tract left inside. When he finally left intensive care for the surgical floor three weeks after the accident, I often found him gazing out the tall windows, looking between the high-rises downtown to the blue water and faint mountains beyond. Intravenous nutrition flowed into his veins from a two-gallon bag hanging above him. He could barely stand on legs weak from his lengthy intensive care stay. I lingered as he talked about a newly built cabin twenty miles down a gravel road, squeezed into a rocky cranny, without running water or electricity. He couldn't wait to get back home. Just him and the new wife. So much setting up to do. The hungry dogs.

On the morning he was finally headed back to Montana, the senior resident said wistfully, "Back to God's country," and Billy Wayne Packer smiled a distant, faraway look. It went to the place inside me where my love for the Montana land lived, where the long forever and ever of Montana highways raced between authoritative mountainsides, a flat stillwater river cut a dark swath through stands of centuries-old evergreens, and something broke open inside. You never knew of land this beautiful.

I wrapped myself in this Montana daydream while I returned to the Seattle wards for a month-long stint on an internal medicine service at the veterans hospital. After Christmas vacation I put my white coat back on and found that patients now thought of me as their primary doctor. Suddenly I had my hands in every stage of medical care, meeting patients in the emergency room when they first arrived, examining them on rounds with the residents and on frequent solo visits through the day, on to their discharge home. Patients began to entrust me with key pieces of information and ask questions of outlook and prognosis. I provided explanations and treatments crafted from what I read in textbooks and what supervising residents taught me in a team room sheltered away from the ward. I could play the doctoring role with some conviction but deep down understood it was still a kind of acting.

At the hospital I was quickly reabsorbed into a hierarchy where medical students were bottom feeders. I belonged to a svelte team of medicine residents and students that operated as a relentless machine, traveling as a pack through the hospital to rounds, teaching conferences, and meals. Under the guidance of an attending doctor, we managed one share of the hospital's business. Every four days we were on call and took care of incoming and hospitalized patients through the day and night. On the post-call morning we presented new patients and plans to the attending and then spent the day carrying out diagnostic tests and treatments. When the work finally finished I went home and slipped into a deep sleep, having been on my feet for as long as thirty-six hours in one stretch. Between call shifts we continued lengthy diagnostic searches, tuned medications, and discharged patients who improved.

My life became one of resigned solitude. I rarely saw good friends, who had rotated at nearby hospitals and kept equally onerous schedules. In the depths of call nights I roamed empty hallways while patients slept, their televisions humming in quiet rooms, a ward clerk tapping forlornly at the front desk. Sleep deprivation settled into my fiber. Days passed seamlessly, with few hints of an outside world. I experienced day-light through dusty windows and stole breaths of the sharp winter air in unheated tunnels between buildings, in parking lots. My love life limited itself to a couple of unanswered crushes. Evenings, I sat at my kitchen table reading of things seen in the hospital.

Moments of clarity emerged on those shifts that stretched across most of two days. Sometimes, in the twenty-sixth or thirtieth hour, a patient's course crystallized in my mind and I shivered with the pleasure of puzzling out the complex biology of human disease. Soon I was on a mad bent to take in all of adult medicine. I honed in on specific tasks like managing a ventilator, tuning up my neurologic exam, learning antibiotics. The month became saturated with these tasks carried out at patients' bedsides and while reading in the team room between conferences and rounds. I had the luck of a spectacular attending physician who spent hours examining heart murmurs and pulses and skin rashes with me and I became impassioned about the body's response to disease. I began identifying patients according to organ dysfunction, and I fractured stories apart into tales of minor diseases and fluctuations in electrolytes and enzymes. By month's end I could disassemble patients' stories into the smallest discrete bits and pieces, turning the parts over in my mind and trying to solve each problem with a reasoned solution. Answers to clinical questions sometimes came spontaneously from accumulated knowledge and I finally functioned with some confidence.

The Seattle month ended abruptly one Friday night when I discharged an aging vet with a green six-pound oxygen tank and physical therapy and blood-thinning injections to be administered at home by a fearless wife. I was due in Montana on Monday morning and had a five-hundred-mile drive ahead of me.

The Montana ground was deep in snow when I arrived late that February weekend, and my tires spun helplessly on streets hardened with ice. For days I moved about in a hazy time warp, my internal life still ticking by the four-day clock of the Seattle wards. I found myself among strangers who engaged in polite conversation, among friendly patients and nurses who passed time with cheerful chatter. I watched detachedly as ordinary people moved through their days. I was lonely for the comfortable academic nest I'd just left behind, that team room off the hospital ward where residents coaxed and encouraged and complimented my care of patients, where solving medical problems was often an exercise of intellectual joy, where in the middle of call nights we compared the best meals we'd eaten in Seattle and our favorite trails in the mountains. I missed the good friends I'd reconnected with briefly after months in WWAMI-land and wondered why I'd had such hasty determination to leave Seattle again. So I trucked through new routines at the Missoula clinic and hospital, tended distractedly to patients, stared wistfully out long windows of the cardiology suite at icy sidewalks and naked sullen trees. Then the human story reasserted itself boldly and swept me to a place I recognized immediately as a place of danger and compromise, where I ought to pay close attention and tread with great care.

Mornings in Missoula began in the dark safety of the radiology suite scrutinizing x-rays with a pulmonologist named Fred Cusack. Cusack was slim and diminutive with a meticulous silver mustache that hid his mouth. He lived on a small farm outside of town where he and his wife raised a stable full of horses. I know he checked on the animals in the early dark mornings, and I imagined him breaking ice in the water basin with the handle of an ax before going to work. At the hospital he wore a fleece vest in lieu of a white coat. His fingernails were short and clean and he walked soundlessly, appearing and disappearing from the wards with little commotion. He had a calmness and warmth with patients that I admired very much, and which probably made him good with horses.

We began our mornings scrolling through x-rays that ran like slow black-and-white documentary films, showing the advent and regression of disease. We scrutinized the images for their portents of recovery and demise as we talked about each hospital patient he followed. One morning, Cusack said that heart surgeons had consulted us about a patient named Martha Stark, who had not woken after an urgent coronary bypass operation and was sustained on life support. He tracked his hospital patients on three-by-five index cards and now pulled Martha's card from the deck, reading of her surgery, diabetes, and failing lungs. He selected her name on the automatic console, and her chest x-rays trundled up and forward on the board. The images suggested worsening lung failure. I sat quietly absorbing the shock of the cloudy haze wrapped around her heart.

After reviewing all of the chest x-rays, we moved upstairs to the intensive care unit, where Martha lay at the center of a gauzy, emotionless calm. Her face was waxy, her hands heavy and swollen and her silver curls sticky with accumulated sweat. I squeezed her damp hand and she opened her eyes but did not look to me. I leaned into her line of sight but she continued her fixed stare, unresponsive to my insistent gaze or the pressure of my hand in hers. In my head I called her name but found I could not manage actual words with my tongue. Finally, forcing my hands to mimic Cusack's, I listened with my stethoscope to crackling that came with every breath. I pushed on ankles that felt like sponges heavy with water. A monitor above the bed showed her heart rhythm tracking evenly and her blood pressure holding strong. Her condition seemed stable despite her strange unresponsiveness.

Cusack stood across the bed from me and we discussed the fluid in her lungs, her failing heart, and treatments to remove excess water from her body. I glanced down from time to time as we talked, wondering if we would rouse her from this state of advanced unconsciousness, and then my thoughts drifted through questions of recovery and survival. I asked Cusack how he thought her course would unfold.

"Hard to say," he replied. He led me out of the room. "In this sort of situation I like to give patients a few days to wake up and start breathing on their own. Sometimes it takes that long to tell. Martha could surprise us. But after a few days without progress, the chance she'll ever come off the ventilator is probably about zero."

Cusack added that he liked to be blunt from the start to

prepare families for anything to happen. We went into the waiting room where Martha's husband, Milo, sat talking on the phone with an expression of extreme concern. Milo hung up the phone hastily and stood to shake our hands. Cusack told Milo that the problems were in her heart and lungs, and that her illness was potentially treatable. Then his voice changed sharply and he said he didn't know why she hadn't woken after surgery, that her unconsciousness might be a more ominous sign. He recommended giving her a few days to recover but if her coma stretched beyond that window, we might want to reconsider life support.

Milo was lanky and tan and his cheeks flushed as he took in the situation. Then he nodded his head a few times and said, "I want you to know something. She is a real lady and a first-class gardener."

Then he fell silent, and I could see that she inhabited his idea of the present as readily as she had a week ago, when she walked out to check the mail or drew the window shades at night, or sat talking with him at the dinner table. Now I realized that in conversation with Cusack, we had only thought of Martha as a body filled with disease.

Cusack said, "I have heard about her garden." Milo flushed again. There was another pause in the conversation and I waited anxiously for Milo to say something or Cusack to continue talking. Finally Cusack told Milo that there was hope for Martha and we would all pray for her. As we left the hospital, Cusack murmured to me that Milo seemed realistic about how sick she was. Cusack seemed comforted by this state of affairs. He mused that there was a better than even chance

Milo would have to eventually decide for Martha about stopping antibiotics, escalating pain medications, and removing the life-sustaining ventilator. He turned to me and said Milo needed time to absorb this possibility.

Martha's health gradually improved over the next few days. Excess fluid came off with diuretics. Her morning chest x-ray cleared. She coughed up phlegm and aired her lungs. One afternoon she opened her eyes and recognized Milo. Cusack ordered the tube removed from her lungs and the ventilator turned off. She sat up with Milo that night holding his hand and watching the television news. Her voice was strained from having the ventilator tubing lodged in her throat, and she was pale from the rigors of illness. Milo walked about the ward with a reserved euphoria.

In the morning while we were on rounds, a nurse named Kim suddenly appeared in the room, clapped a hand to Cusack's shoulder, and said, "Could you come right away please—Martha Stark needs your help."

Cusack stopped midsentence, pardoned himself, and turned automatically to the door.

In the room, bright ceiling lights shone down on Martha, who now lay flat on her back.

"Squeeze my hand, Martha!" a nurse said, hovering a few inches above Martha's face. Four nurses were at work around the bed, peeling back blankets and clothing and setting IVs. Her skin had turned the gray of plaster and her eyes opened in that familiar vacant stare. As Martha reached toward her heart, a nurse swiftly pinned and tied her wrist to the bed, as if roping a calf.

In a loud, unfamiliar voice Cusack said, "What happened?"

"She was watching television after breakfast and suddenly became unresponsive."

"Vital signs?" Heads turned as he maneuvered to the head of the bed.

"O$_2$ sat's in the fifties," Kim said. "Pressure's 100."

"She have a pulse?" Cusack said.

"Good pulse," said a nurse pushing two gloved fingers roughly against Martha's neck. Another swabbed at Martha's wrist and drew brackish blood from the artery.

"Heart rate's 135."

Cusack pointed at me. "Listen to her lungs," he directed.

Suddenly I saw that Martha's chest did not move. I watched the color of her lips fade to gray and then blue. Kim pushed a suction catheter deeply into Martha's nostril. Phlegm came back through the clean narrow tubing in thick clumps. I leaned down to listen. No breath sounds came to my ears and I felt her chest remain in that horrifying, motionless repose. Now I realized that she was dying and I broke out in a sweat. I listened for what seemed many moments, my hand pressing the stethoscope hard against her chest, and I concentrated to pick up any noise at all. Her wrists rattled in the cloth restraints, and suddenly I realized she might still be conscious at some level, aware that she couldn't get a breath in, pinned down terrifyingly, unable to fight back.

Cusack reached in to listen to her lungs, moving his stethoscope rapidly over four points that suggested a square. He straightened quickly and accepted a metal blade and clear tube from Kim. Now he moved as though motorized, efficiently filling every moment with action. In one swift motion he pressed the blade to Martha's tongue, lifted her chin, and slid the tube into her windpipe. I heard the hiss and sigh of the ventilator as the tubing was attached together. Cusack said, "Can I have a bronchoscope please."

"Three minutes," said a nurse in back, who had been scribbling a record of events.

I stepped back, my fingers curling automatically and my fingernails digging into my palms. Cusack tucked his necktie into his vest. A nurse pushed a small syringe of morphine through Martha's IV, to calm her. Kim handed Cusack the bronchoscope and he fed the slim black tube through the ventilator tubing. Martha began to cough and her body bucked and lifted off the bed. Her arms struggled against the restraints. Cusack pressed one eye to the bronchoscope screen, feet planted firmly, face perfectly composed, guiding the tube down its familiar path into her windpipe and deeper into the pink and still airways. He turned the scope's wheels backward and forward with three agile fingers. Then a rush of noise came from the depths of her body and Cusack yanked the bronchoscope back in one swift, slippery movement. A thick clot of blood and mucus was attached to the end of the scope. Numbly, I watched Martha pull in a deep breath. Kim emitted a loud sigh and reached into her back pocket for tape to secure the ventilator tubing. Martha's chest rose and the ventilator sighed with a long fresh breath. Above the bed, the cardiac monitor broadcast an oxygen saturation of 72 percent. I watched as the numbers blinked 81-82-81 percent and then up to 88 percent, and her gray skin brightened to pink.

"Four and a half minutes," said the nurse in back.

"One more pressure," Cusack said.

"One-fifty over eighty-four," Kim said.

"Please send the usual labs," he said, ticking off a list of blood tests.

Cusack turned away from the bed, shook the bloody clot into the trash can, and carefully put the instrument in the sink. Turning, he bent to listen to Martha's lungs again, then straightened and said, "Thank you, everybody. I think we're done." The nurses moved to straighten Martha's body, slip on her hospital gown, replace blankets. For a few moments I watched Martha breathe calmly, fully unaware of what had just happened.

When I turned toward the hall my eyes locked with Milo's. He was standing in front of the nurses' desk and he looked overwhelmed with panic. Only then did I realize he had watched the full resuscitation through her window. I considered how he might have felt watching heroics thrust on Martha, the rude maneuvers on her body, the businesslike air in the room, probes pushed deeply down her throat and chest. Cusack suddenly materialized next to me, still using every moment to move and speak, as though the resuscitation had not yet ended.

"Milo," Cusack said. As they shook hands he continued, "She had a plug in her lungs and stopped breathing for about a minute. We got that plug out of there as quickly as we could but she had to go back on the machine. It's a setback. I was so hopeful that she would stay off." Cusack sighed and then added, "I think we may have a pretty good idea of where she's headed." Now Milo's face rearranged itself into a hundred questions.

What came out of his mouth was, "Should I call people to come?" His eyes roved warily between Cusack and me.

Cusack's face changed and then his voice dropped back to its soft, natural timbre. "Yes, have them come," he said.

"Soon?"

"Yes, soon."

Cusack was quiet crossing the street to the clinic in the bright sunshine. Finally he said, "That was scary. I thought we were going to lose her right then."

Then I realized Cusack had already imagined Martha's death and fixed on a very specific vision of her dying. I realized he did not wish anybody to die that graceless, choking death and go out surrounded by strangers, a stunned and aggrieved husband watching helplessly through the window. My thoughts drifted to medicine residents in Seattle stewing over a patient's course, their inexhaustible attempts to stabilize patients, the primeval desperation when things soured. Nothing in the world compared to that sensation of things going wrong suddenly and unpredictably and irreversibly, without a chance for dignified dying, without last acts of comfort.

By morning I knew what to make of Martha's condition. On our rounds she was again suspended in a deep unconsciousness. Her eyes had shut heavily and her body lay motionless beneath the bedsheets. When Cusack and I studied the nursing notes, we saw that she had consumed increasing amounts of oxygen through the night, that she'd fallen into such a deep coma that she hadn't needed sedatives or pain medication to blunt the ventilator experience. Cusack turned to the machine and told me she had ceased to breathe independently, that her lung functions now depended entirely on the machine.

"Listen," he said, facing me. He switched off the ventilator for a few moments and I gasped. He motioned for silence. I held my breath waiting for her to draw a spontaneous breath of her own, but her chest lay oddly still again. The monitor above the bed showed her oxygen level dropping slowly. After fifteen seconds he flipped the switch again and a long controlled breath rolled down the moist plastic tubing into her lungs.

I felt icy shivers pass through my body. Now I knew how tenuous Martha's grasp on life was, having witnessed her near death and gradual decline in the aftermath of the previous day's indignant resuscitation, how she ceased to breathe off the machine. I'd learned to fear the capricious powers of the human body to act as it wished, regardless of what the mind hoped for. I had watched life unwind from Martha bit by bit. I had confidence that we could keep her body alive for a time, that we had tools to resist physical dying. But I believed now that she would never talk with Milo again and would never recognize him or touch him meaningfully. Urgently I wanted Cusack to announce the prognosis we had stepped carefully around. When I looked up, Milo was standing in the doorway and Cusack went immediately to him.

Milo said, "We need to talk."

When we went into the conference room later that day, Milo looked squarely at me and nodded. He put his arm around Cusack's shoulders and Cusack, looking up in surprise, returned the gesture. Martha's middle-aged children filed into the room and sat around a long cluttered table. The children became teary as Cusack described the aggressive process in her lungs that hadn't responded to our treatments. Martha had virtually no chance of coming off life support, he said. When he paused, heads turned to Milo. Milo was soft-spoken, definitive, dry-eyed. I imagined that he had spent the day drifting around in prior decades, combing his memory for things he had forgotten to say, moments he meant to explain. His thoughts had drifted through the small good moments they had shared in forty years of knowing each other. Trying to remember in case he had the chance for a last word, trying to remember so he would never forget. He put his hands gently on the table, sighed, and said, "I know she wouldn't want to go on like this." When we walked out of the meeting, I was still trying not to cry.

The following morning I woke thinking about how Martha was going to die that day. I got out of the warm bed reluctantly to face new snow on the ground, an icy windshield, Cusack's morning rounds, the gleaming ICU. When the chosen hour arrived, Martha's sons and daughters crowded around the bed in a tight circle. A nurse brushed Martha's curls off her forehead and onto the pillow in a smooth silver wave. Two grandchildren twisted and whispered in the doorway. Milo sat with her and rubbed her heavy hands. Kim, the ICU nurse, called to the clinic with news that Martha died ten minutes after the ventilator was turned off.

"That was the best thing," Cusack said softly. Later I realized he might be speaking not only for her but also for himself. I had seen him twice with patients who died so quickly that no one had time to say goodbye. I would watch him bring parents, spouses, children to face unexpected situations and usually under considerable time pressure. At first I could see only the artistry with which he handled such situations. Gradually I saw how affected he was by small failures between humans at the end of life, the tragedy of seeing people not speak in time. I could see now why we had tried from the beginning to predict the future, to prepare Milo and his family for this most difficult and protracted human process.

Now I had seen doctoring performed with great care and come to understand the profession as something much more complex than language and gestures, than a simple actor's repertoire. What Cusack offered his patients drew on everything he'd seen and known in twenty years of his patients fighting and recovering and living and dying.

Eventually Martha's death floated quietly away from me. In the end there wasn't much left to mull over. We had done everything we could and I believed we had resisted the temptation to do too much. I knew Milo believed this to be true, too. Above all, Martha's wishes had been honored and she had died in peace.

There was such a thing as dying a good death. I had been lucky enough to watch it unfold.

Left to my own devices, I wanted revolution. I wanted patients to snap off their televisions, quit smoking, protect their homes with dogs rather than guns, and ease down from the excesses of the American diet. Health, I believed, came from breathing fresh air, walking, eating vegetables,

sleeping well, and kindness between people. Internal medicine seemed the perfect human laboratory for my optimism, a
setting where patients could make real choices about diseases
that would simmer and flare over an entire adult life, where
a doctor's advice might make a difference over many years.
I especially did not want to become the sort of doctor who
liberally tossed pills at patients, and I took this mission very
seriously. I had discovered I could use a patient's hospitalization as a pulpit to teach what I had learned.

Naturally, the situations didn't often play out how I
expected, and I stumbled comically trying to imitate the
smooth, reassuring ways of experienced attending doctors
with their patients.

I was in the clinic with a general internist named Katharine
McDermott when the emergency room called about a young
woman named Susie Culver, who had just checked in with
trouble breathing.

"You've got some business," McDermott said briskly, hanging up the phone and handing me an index card where she'd
written Susie's name and record number. McDermott was
small, sturdy, and athletic. She had come to Missoula straight
from residency and over several years had built a large successful practice on a reputation for clarity and honesty and
concern for patients' well-being. She was busy enough that
in addition to a full clinic load, she usually attended to a few
hospital patients as well. Often, she sent me on reconnais-
sance to the hospital.

"Why don't you go over and have a look at Susie. She
has asthma," she said, adding that she would meet me after

wrapping up the day's clinic load. I took Susie's card readily from her, eager to work out the diagnosis and management myself. As I went out the door, McDermott smiled wryly and said, "Be careful, she just about died on me once."

I felt alert crossing the bright snowy street and instructed myself to assess Susie's condition quickly. I ran through the things I should check in the first few moments of meeting her: her oxygen level, the cadence of breaths, signs of worsening breathing. Then I came through automatic doors at the top of the ambulance ramp. The emergency department swirled with doctors, medics, and nurses. A tall display board behind the main desk listed eight active patients. Magnets placed next to the names reported progress: "Triage," "Labs," "Surgery," the labels read. A rush of adrenaline came into me.

A magnet next to Susie's name said "X-ray" and I went to a light board in the inner hallway where her chest films hung. I traced the silhouette of her heart as it disappeared behind a hazy shadow. Then I realized I could hear her raspy breaths and went quickly into the room, reminding myself of what to check.

Susie was a redhead with a spiky ponytail and a fine spray of freckles over her nose. She lifted her shoulders sharply when she inhaled, touching her throat and chest nervously to conjure slow, deep breaths. Alarmed, I thought, *Is she going to crash?* I glanced into the hall for a nurse or attending who might be passing by and thought of things we might require to revive her.

Susie looked anxiously at me, then broke the silence, saying, "I have asthma."

I thought, *She can speak and make sense and probably won't crash, but she doesn't look good.* I glanced at the chart. She was thirty-one years old and her oxygen level was adequate with extra oxygen from a thin tube blowing air to her nose.

Momentarily reassured, I introduced myself and said, "What happened?"

Susie said the attack had started while vacuuming a client's house. Puffs on an inhaler did not clear the tightness in her lungs, and she went out for fresh air. She ran a housecleaning business, she explained, so she had to stay to finish the job. Afterward, a clinic nurse sent her along to the emergency room. She told this history in bursts, words coming in pressured couplets and triplets between breaths, and she finished sentences with hand waving. I listened with my stethoscope and heard air squealing and straining to escape the swollen, inflamed airways. Her heart beat faintly, the sounds muffled by air trapped in her lungs.

A nurse came in the room now, squirted solution into the nebulizer basin, attached the oxygen hose, and handed the treatment to Susie. She took the pipe in her mouth. I sat down in the room and began writing hospital orders. Before I was done with the page of orders, Susie's breathing settled measurably. Then I began to think of what we would do for her in the hospital. The most likely scenario was that pneumonia, seen on the chest x-ray, had triggered an asthma attack. I requested antibiotics for the infection and inhaled medications to open airways, steroids for inflammation, and oxygen as needed. Any medical cookbook like the well-used one I carried in my white coat pocket packaged asthma attacks in just this way, I knew. I wrote methodically into the chart, pressing strongly so the orders would copy through three sheets.

I went out and found McDermott, who had just arrived. She sat on top of the nursing desk facing me and nodded frequently as I told of ineffective inhalers, Susie's clipped sentences, tight wheezy lungs. I mentioned the chest x-ray shadow and laid out my plan. Susie had been intubated and ventilated for several days once, I added, and any asthma attack had the potential for treachery.

"What's a thirty-year-old doing on a ventilator?" she asked, as she signed my orders.

I did not think of this as a rhetorical question and earnestly said, "She has severe asthma."

McDermott smiled. "Severe asthma is a treatable disease. Nobody should die from an asthma attack in this day and age, yet it happens all the time. Why is that?"

"I guess they could have taken medications incorrectly," I said.

"And what else? What triggers asthma attacks?"

I reeled off a list of common allergies and mentioned Susie's work in dusty houses.

"You see the point," she said, interrupting me impatiently. "It's not like we do anything all that different here in the hospital. You've prescribed the same basic medications that she's already supposed to be taking. I guarantee she'll get better here. So why didn't all this stuff work for her at home?"

I didn't think I could answer this question in a way that would please her and finally I said I wasn't sure.

"Think about it tonight," she said as we left the hospital at day's end.

In the morning I arrived with a full speech about preventing asthma attacks. My advice for Susie involved a rigorous schedule of inhalers plus a warning against cat hair and house dust. This would probably mean she would have to switch jobs. I went into Susie's hospital room prepared to deliver the speech and found her sitting forward in bed, exhaling hoarsely. Her cheeks had flushed bright pink and her eyes were wide with alarm. My heart fluttered in my chest. A nurse hurried into the room with a breathing treatment. I glanced at the chart, which recorded oxygen levels of 95 percent to 98 percent that morning. Susie's breathing began to calm after several misty puffs. I clamped the oxygen sensor onto her index finger and the level popped up at 96 percent.

When McDermott appeared on the ward, she listened to Susie's story all the way through and then said, "Five milligrams of diazepam. Let's see how that works."

I paused with surprise. "Valium? Won't that suppress her breathing?"

"That's basically what you want, to slow down her breathing. She's getting plenty of oxygen. What's driving the problem at this point is her anxiety. It's common with asthmatics. The sensation that you can't breathe is very scary, and self-perpetuating."

I was distracted in the clinic all day stewing over Susie's stagnating course. The sedative would stifle her discomfort, I felt, and would not treat her disease. But we had no other cards to play, having already offered everything in the cookbook. All that we could do now was continue with nebulizers and steroids at high doses and stave off her lung failure while the inflammation in her airways gradually subsided. My speech itched inside me, and that evening I returned to the hospital to check on her.

From the open doorway, Susie grinned at me. She was reading from a stack of papers, her legs crossed at the ankles and fluffy red booties on her feet. Oprah rambled on a television high in the corner of the room.

"I feel a hundred percent better," she said. Relieved, I went cautiously into the room.

"You look more comfortable," I said.

"I'm ready to go home," she said. "Think I can go tonight?"

"I think, since it took a day and a half to get control over your asthma, you ought to stay one more night and let's make sure you're completely better."

Susie's eyes flickered upward. "Okay."

"I'd hate for you to come right back here."

"I know, I know," Susie said. "I have been here a few times."

I plunged into my speech about the inhalers, explaining how each worked in the lungs and why a rigorous schedule would prevent future attacks. Susie listened tolerantly, and I continued on about house dust and cat hair and other allergy triggers.

"I graduate in a year and a half," she said, cutting me off. "I'll work as a psychologist then. I just really need to keep my job right now. The money's good. I'm paying for school and I just can't take another loan."

Susie's acute situation was suddenly over, I realized, and this was the tenuous resolution. She would leave in the morning breathing normally and feeling well. That was worth something, even if it was a limited success. But the long view was that Susie would probably have attacks again in a dusty home. One of the attacks might spin out of control and she would end up on a ventilator or die without prompt medical attention. This prospect absolutely terrified me. I wished I could keep her hospitalized indefinitely, and I felt chastened that I couldn't convince her of the grave danger dusty houses posed for her. For weeks afterward when McDermott sent me to the emergency room to meet patients, I worried that I would find Susie sitting bolt upright, her skin blue and cool, eyes flung open with fear. I couldn't prevent that from happening, and this dissatisfied me greatly.

Later I realized that Susie and I were close in age and educational circumstance, but that I really hadn't understood her point of view. I had never gotten sick enough to warrant hospitalization and didn't have a waxing and waning illness that interfered with the way I wished to live. Then I remembered a story that Cusack had told me about hounding patients to quit smoking. In his youth he had cracked down hard and really pissed people off, he said, with harangues about cigarette smoke. Over time he found these patients didn't come back to doctors, and he considered this a failure. His hard approach had not convinced anyone, he said, and he lost every further opportunity to help his patients.

I told McDermott afterward about the determined conversation I'd had with Susie.

"We've definitely been through that," McDermott said. "Did she say she'd change jobs?"

I shook my head and said, "It was pretty frustrating." Suddenly I realized that I might choose similarly if I were in

Susie's position. If I had moderately severe asthma, would I give up running in the cold mountains? Would I stop snow skiing, which could trigger an asthma attack? It would be hard to live such a controlled life. Maybe I would take my chances like Susie did.

"I know it's frustrating," McDermott said. "Sometimes all you can do is let them choose."

When I came into lung clinic one afternoon, Cusack stood from his desk and went straight to the light board in a corner of the back office. He switched the lights on.

"A middle-aged guy comes in complaining of a dry cough. What do you see?"

I scanned the three chest x-rays and pointed to a bulge above the aorta.

"Right," he said. He pulled the chest films down and put up a series of CT scan images. I studied these and pointed to a star-shaped mass that corresponded with the x-rays.

"There it is," I said.

"Yes," he said evenly. "There are a couple spots in there. Scary, very scary. So I bronched him last week. The tumor looked like a walnut. It bled like stink."

"Has the pathology come back?"

Cusack handed me the report. I skimmed descriptions of the specimen and fixatives and red-hued stains, the brute language detailing the distortion inside walls of cells. The pathologist had summarized his report with the conclusion, "Primary lung adenocarcinoma."

"He's checking in right now," Cusack said.

Haltingly, I said, "You're going to tell him."

"Yes."

"Does he have any idea?"

"He has a pretty good idea," Cusack said. "He's pretty realistic. Smoked forty years. But a healthy guy otherwise."

We talked about lung cancer for a moment, about curing adenocarcinoma with surgery if caught before it spread. I looked carefully at the CT scan.

"You said something about a second spot?" I asked.

"Right," Cusack said.

"So no cure," I said.

"It's on the opposite lung," Cusack said. "So surgery's not an option. We won't mention surgery." Suddenly the sound of laughter came through the walls and a door opened then closed.

Cusack's wife, Liz, a beautiful woman with very short hair, looked in. She was officially the business manager but pitched in doing odd jobs from time to time. Today she was checking blood pressures and oxygen levels and bringing patients into exam rooms.

"John Davis and his wife are here," she said, passing the chart to Cusack.

Cusack's voice suddenly tightened.

"How are they doing?"

"You know, chatty, pleasant. Same as usual," she said and chuckled. "John went on for a while about a ride they took this morning. Horses were calm in the snow. He flushed a bunch of quail. He thinks it means spring is coming."

"I think they know," she added carefully.

When we came in the room, John and Ginny stood energetically and the room had the feel of laughter just fading. John wore a heavy canvas jacket the color of honey and his hands were large, warm, and rough.

"Hello, hello," Ginny said. She held a dark leather purse, straps dangling. Her nails were neatly cut. The healthy coloring to their faces suggested long days in the sun.

"Good to see you," Cusack said, shaking hands.

We all sat down and Cusack arranged himself to face John and Ginny directly. I heard every noise in the room: chairs scratching the thin carpet, a hum from incandescent bulbs overhead, sleeves and jeans brushing against each other. Ginny settled in and wrapped her arm over the back of John's chair. John sat forward, hands clasped between legs. His feet were planted solidly in thick boots. Then all of the noise subsided. Footsteps outside the door came and went. I saw that Cusack had left his stethoscope and John's chart in the back office.

"I'm afraid I've got bad news," Cusack said. Ginny closed her eyes and sucked in a deep breath.

"It is cancer," he said. John looked at the ground, then turned to Ginny, whose wide brown eyes were stunned and shiny.

Finally John sat straight and said, "We had a feeling."

"Yes," Ginny said. "John has been on leave." John was a pilot who made his career flying with the Air Force, then switched to freight planes about the same time the children grew up and moved out.

Ginny sighed again and looked at Cusack.

"I am going to give you some information," Cusack said. He spoke slowly, considering each word first. "I am giving you this information so you know what can happen and so we can make decisions together."

"Yes, absolutely," Ginny said.

"We want you to be straight with us," John said, and I realized that it was his rich baritone voice that had filled the room and hung in the air so warmly.

Cusack continued, "The main tumor is on the left lung. It has also gone to a spot on the right lung. We don't have evidence that it's gone anywhere else."

Ginny, listening raptly, said, "But it has spread."

"Yes," Cusack said. "It's spread."

Ginny grasped at John's arm and he glanced her way, the twist of his mouth expressing disbelief and horror. I felt like I was watching a crime being committed.

Cusack continued, "What does all this mean? If we let the cancer run its course, you would probably live nine months. That's if we did nothing at all, no treatment, nothing. Of course, you could live five years. You could die tonight. No one has this kind of information."

I stole a look at John, who listened raptly, and realized I had been holding my breath.

"The treatment we have is chemotherapy, to shrink the tumors and extend your life. You can expect another six or eight months of life from chemotherapy. I know it doesn't sound like much but it could actually double your survival."

"So there's no cure," Ginny said.

"No cure," Cusack said.

John put his hands together and looked straight at Cusack. In that wonderful rich voice he said, "Let's get this show on the road."

Coming to work a few weeks later I passed Ginny in the parking lot. John was receiving chemotherapy at the cancer center and Ginny reported that the first two rounds had gone well.

"His spirits have been terrific, better than I ever imagined," she said, her voice glossy and bright. I pictured him sitting back in the upholstered recliners and joking with his wife while the potent electric yellow fluid ran into his veins. "We're hopeful of a real improvement with the chemo."

"That's great, glad to hear it." My voice came out dry and reedy.

Then no news came until Liz Cusack called as my rotation was ending. "Dr. Cusack wanted you to know that John and Ginny Davis are coming in tomorrow," she said. "He just had the follow-up chest CT." She said the appointment would be at three o'clock. I said I would come over then.

"Have you seen John?" I asked.

"He hasn't been in since that day," Liz said. "Bill Oakland's mainly managing his care right now. But I hear he's been pretty sick and tired from chemo." Oakland was the oncologist who prescribed chemotherapy.

"Not that surprising."

"No, but it's always awful to hear," she said. There was a pause and then she added, "They are a lovely couple."

The CT scan sat on the shelf in the back office when I came in the next day. I opened the envelope warily and hung the films on the light board. The images looked almost identical to the first images we had seen. Cusack came in a moment later, took a cursory look at the board, and dropped a stack of charts on his desk.

"Looks about the same," I said.

"Yes, exactly," Cusack said. "Oakland talked to them yesterday, so they know the news."

While Cusack finished some paperwork I mulled over the scans, feeling sick thinking of the visit ahead. We would offer even more aggressive treatment that would add no more than a few months' survival and was toxic with side effects. We did not have good choices left, I knew, and I dreaded hearing Cusack say so.

John and Ginny were murmuring when we came in. They stood and greeted us, and I saw they were both tired. The feeling in the room was muted. I closed the door softly. John relaxed in his chair, leaned back, and put his arm around his wife. She smiled at me, then John, then Cusack.

"How are you folks doing?" Cusack asked.

"We were surprised by the news," John said. "Dr. Oakland called last night as soon as he had the results."

Cusack shifted in his chair.

"He told us that the tumor had not really shrunk," John said.

"I've seen the films," Cusack said. "That's the truth. The tumor is about the same as before."

"Ginny and I talked about it for a long time last night. The chemo just wipes me out and my appetite's shot."

I imagined them sitting together late in the evening,

watching a log cracking and sparking in the fireplace, embers glowing white, a shower of ashes flaring up in the dark. Maybe they talked about thirty-five years together, children on the brink of new families, a ranch flush with young horses. The dog shook himself and came whistling and grumbling into the room, circled once in front of the fire, and climbed on the couch to curl up next to John. For the first time in weeks, John felt alert and they talked late, coming finally to the pressing decision.

"We've lost whole weeks to that chemo," Ginny said.

"So we decided that that's it. No more chemo," John said. He waved his hand sharply, a gesture of finality.

"We feel very certain," Ginny said.

"Hold up," Cusack said abruptly, sitting forward. "What did Oakland say?"

"He suggested a more aggressive kind of chemo," John said.

Cusack murmured, "Right. I've talked with him. He thinks it would give you a few more good months."

There was a long silence in the room and finally Ginny said, "We're going to go back to the ranch and enjoy our lives, have one more wonderful summer."

I looked at Cusack and saw in his eyes that the negotiation was over.

Now John said, "I just want to ride the horses a few more times." His voice lit up the quiet room.

A faint smile came across Cusack's lips.

"Ride horses my whole life," John said to Ginny, his tone turned happy and foolish, and they laughed together. "Every chance I get."

After work that evening I ran to the high plateau at the end of town, going up a long road past new housing construction stunted by unexpected snowfall. I was suddenly happy thinking of the days starting to lengthen. The road continued on in the golden late-day light, turning to gravel and diving under thick evergreen cover. I felt myself storing away the day's events and my mind cleared in the cold dry air. I had been running for some time and now I slowed to watch the light change, the wide sky going blue then purple. A wisp of evening mist floated down over a mountain ridge and curled around a stand of ponderosa pines. Such beauty and simplicity. I stopped, hoping for a little of everything to seep inside. Finally as stars appeared one by one, I turned toward home.

As I came down the long hill, I felt a strange gladness for John and his decision to stop chemotherapy and get on with the living he had left. It was probably the bravest thing I'd ever heard from a patient. I believed he could stomach the days ahead, that he could weather the inevitable decline, and he was ready to tackle the unknown of dying. But I didn't think he had capitulated. He wanted cold air and he wanted the sound of hooves pounding rough ground, the smell of dirt, his body moving inseparably with the mare like his most primitive instinct. He wanted to run full stride in the open range, the mare snorting and humid.

The thought of horses hit me in a way so beautiful I knew I hadn't thought of horses that way before.

I believed he would get through summer without a hitch. He would revel in the hot land again in all its glory, and I hoped he would make it through fall to enjoy the long beautiful gold light one more time. I wondered if the horses would know he was dying. I wondered if their world would change when he didn't come around in the morning anymore. I hoped Ginny would never feel alone and I felt certain their deep strengths would carry them along.

McDermott stood next to her desk holding a thick chart. She tapped a pen against the day's schedule, moved her lips from side to side, studied me a moment, then handed over the hefty blue chart.

"Velma Carter is here for a diabetes recheck," she said. I opened the chart and saw she had come to the doctor faithfully every three months.

Now I followed McDermott into the clinic hallway, which had twenty patient rooms up and down the long narrow corridor that were shared among internists, a gastroenterologist, and a pulmonologist. She went into an open doorway and said, "Hello Velma." I heard a chair scrape against the floor inside the room, but I couldn't see the patient.

"Doctor."

"I'd like my medical student to visit with you first, if that's alright. She'd like to talk to you about diabetes."

A raspy voice in the room said, "Well, bring her in."

McDermott twisted around and said mischievously, "Don't let her give you a hard time." She steered me into the room.

At first glance, Velma was a leathery woman wearing jeans and a fleece jacket. The chart set her age at sixty-eight years. Her hands felt thick and rough and ancient. I shut the door of the small room and sat down facing her.

"So you're a medical student, an MD-to-be," Velma said, chuckling. "How many years until you're a real doctor?"

"Another year of medical school and three years of residency," I said.

"Long ways to go."

"Yes," I said.

"Where you from?"

I told her and explained that the medical school sent us to work in small towns all over the Pacific Northwest.

"You been to Missoula before?"

"A few times, and it seems like a great town."

"I'll tell you, I just bought six acres down on the Bitterroot River. You know the Bitterroot? Beautiful. Just absolutely beautiful. Fought off three other people trying to get that land. Six months later one guy comes back and offers me double what I paid for the place. I told him no way. I have a little house for just me. My husband's passed away. We were homesteaders up in Alaska, moved up there in the fifties to get our land. We grew everything you could think of, squash, corn, beans, you name it. But it's a hard life and we got old. I guess I didn't feel like hanging around Alaska much longer after he died. But Montana suits me fine."

I liked the way the conversation was going and I said, "What do you like to do with yourself?"

"Well, crocheting is for grannies! I like to travel, now that my knee's better. I just got back from Yellowstone on one of those big buses. You been there?"

"I'd like to go. Did you see buffalo?"

"Saw a lot of buffalo. Lot of 'em dead." That winter there

had been a brucellosis epidemic and ranchers were in an uproar about buffalo crossing out of the national park and passing the disease on to cattle. Velma waved her arm in a wide arc to demonstrate a field covered with dead and dying buffalo.

"What a big mess," I said.

"Big animals," she said.

"Sounds like you're weathering the winter just fine."

"I'm not one of these grannies that flees to Arizona for the winter. But I'm ready for spring. I'm ready to get things planted. I keep a big garden and I still plant sweet corn. I get a lot of deer. They know where I live and they love the young lettuce, so I find I have to drop a buck every now and then. Deer are such pests."

"You keep a gun?" The medical student in me was suddenly paying attention, recalling the study we had read in epidemiology class that showed a household gun was used against the owner three times as often as against the intruder.

"Several guns. I keep them clean and I keep the rifle handy."

I must have had a certain look on my face, because she said, "Young lady, I can handle a gun just fine. Now what can I do for you today?"

"Why don't you talk to me about the diabetes."

"Oh, all these damned pills," she said. "I forget to take the pills sometimes. Do you think I need to be on all these pills?"

"Let's start with the basics," I said. "Are you checking your blood sugar?"

"When I remember," she said.

"Do you write it down? Did you bring in the numbers?"

"Guess I forgot," she said.

I sucked a deep breath in and said, "Any problems with numbness or tingling in your feet or hands?"

"Doc said that would happen if my blood sugar was high. But no numbness."

"Any problems with your eyes?"

"Just the usual problems."

"Which are . . . "

"Bad eyesight." She pointed to her glasses.

"Do you check your feet?"

"I check my feet."

I hesitated while I searched for my next question and she said, "I skip my pills sometimes. That vitamin has a vile taste." She reached under her chair and handed me a brown paper bag filled with pharmacy bottles. I stood and poured the bag's contents on the exam table. There were two medications to control blood sugar, one for heartburn, one for blood pressure and kidneys, a giant bottle of aspirin, and vitamins. She had six medications in total and two had to be taken twice daily. I opened the nearly full bottle of vitamins. The pills were brown and oblong, and a single pill looked big enough to make a grown woman stop breathing if it lodged in the wrong place.

I reached for the chart and read Velma's vital signs. Today's blood pressure was 135/89, which was borderline high and would not mix particularly well with her diabetes, I knew. I asked her about exercise.

"Sure," she said. "I walk every day. Not like those folks who like to put on spandex and lipstick and try not to sweat.

I'm around the property, checking on things and clearing branches. I stay active."

I directed Velma up to the exam table. She talked about the snowpack and the long winter while I felt for lymph nodes and pressed on her abdomen, and as I felt the careful, even pulses in her feet. Then I told her I would return with McDermott and a plan for the diabetes.

"I doubt we can stop the medications," I said. "They're all important."

I went out of the room and sat on McDermott's couch thinking of what I wanted to do for Velma. In the office I reviewed her past year of laboratory results and found her blood sugars elevated at every visit; the average ran quite a bit higher than normal but still below the level predicting kidney, eye, and nerve damage. McDermott's prior notes indicated that Velma had never taken her medication regularly and I realized that I was unlikely to improve her erratic medication use either. So much for revolution.

Then I considered what I really wanted for Velma, and that was for her to live as many healthy years on the Bitterroot stake as she could. I especially wanted her to live without foot numbness, without pressure sores that became infected and spread up her foot. I didn't want deteriorating health to force her to live somewhere that would eviscerate the spirit in her. Her medication mattered some in the big picture, but it didn't mean everything.

I'd just had a conversation with my Seattle housemate, who had called, laughing, to ask if she could sell me any drugs. She had rotated onto the Harborview internal medicine service where, in addition to the fast-paced ward routine, medical students were swallowing a daily regimen of four medications at the behest of the chief medical resident. She had begun taking the pills faithfully, sugar tabs and vitamins meant to represent treatments for heart disease and diabetes, or HIV. Within a few days she'd found it impossible to stay on a schedule that required dosing three times daily. She said her strategy now was to sell the medications like some patients did, and she hoped it would appear she had adhered to the drug regimen. Then we talked about how patients could possibly take ten and twenty medications per day with any degree of accuracy and we wondered what fraction of patients truly complied with their medications. A schedule of ten medications could control your entire day if you wanted to do it right.

McDermott came in her office and set a chart on her desk. She scratched out two new prescriptions for another patient while I talked about Velma. When I finished she said, "So Velma's the same."

"I suppose so."

"Did you see this morning's labs?" She reached behind her and took a slip of pink carbon paper from a remote pile. I studied the numbers, which showed that her average blood glucose for the past three months had dropped back into the normal range.

"This is a change," I said, puzzled.

"Something worked."

I nodded vigorously. "I wonder what she did."

McDermott started laughing and said, "Maybe she's taking her medication. Maybe she's eating better. Or maybe she's doing more strenuous activity now that her knee's healed. Those are nice-looking numbers. What's she on?"

"Glyburide five milligrams twice daily, and metformin one gram twice daily."

"What do you want to do for her?"

"She asked if we would stop some of her medications. But I guess I would leave her doses where they are. If her sugars stay controlled, we could think about stopping glyburide next time."

"Exactly. We'd like to know that this wasn't just a chance event. We'd like to know what happens over time. Should we go talk with her?"

"Sure."

McDermott said, "Maybe Velma will even go for the plan this time."

Carla Runyon told me earnestly one afternoon that she was thinking of suing her hometown doctor for malpractice. She said this in a way that made me think she'd already told the story to an attentive lawyer with a yellow legal pad. Carla was a college sophomore and her medical chart was dense with photographs, lab reports, and progress notes that corroborated the long story of her mysterious illness. Three years had elapsed since she'd been to the doctor in her hometown of four thousand. In that time she'd had emergency surgery to save her life and the cryptic diagnosis was nailed down. Meanwhile she had moved to Missoula and become a clinic patient of Dr. McDermott's, but the story was still fresh in her mind.

When I met Carla, she was curled on a gurney in a dark room off the emergency department hallway, the brim of a baseball hat pulled level with her eyebrows. She had spent two days trying to convince her gastroenterologist she was having severe stomach pain and he had advised her to take more medication at home. Finally she had come defiantly to the ER when her pain remained unbearable, and the specialist had groaned when he heard. Her boyfriend handed me a basin of teal-colored vomit when I walked in. I didn't know what to do with the basin so I tilted it from side to side and watched the bright fluid, the color of a robin's egg, spread thinly across the bottom. A half-digested pill surfaced then disappeared as the fluid splashed and pooled in a corner. I handed the basin back to her boyfriend, who put it down and pushed it away with his foot.

Carla closed her eyes. Speaking softly and reluctantly, she seemed almost elderly with exhaustion. She talked of stabbing pains in her belly and vomiting that had cleaned out everything except the thinnest bile. She hadn't eaten regular food in two days. At first her diarrhea had been worse than usual and then had subsided completely.

She opened her eyes and became a twenty-year-old again, her gaze locking onto mine. She said, "I've had Crohn's disease for four years."

"Crohn's," I said, rummaging through memory for information that might be of use. "Is this what your flares are like?"

"No, this is worse," she said. "Usually they get better in a day or two if I take extra sulfasalazine."

When she pushed back her shirt, her belly was slim and

pale. A zipperlike scar ran down the middle of her abdomen, pink and raised. The scar curved out around her belly button. I placed my hands on her smooth skin and pushed against the supple abdominal muscles. Below the liver I felt a firm knot of intestine that loosened reluctantly with pressure from my fingertips. Carla tensed, groaned, rolled from side to side under my hands.

"That's been there a couple days," she said and pushed her hands along the knot.

After I finished the examination I said, "We'll bring you into the hospital, get some fluids going, start up medications."

She grimaced and rolled toward the wall. I retreated with her thick chart, perused photographs of the interior of her colon, shiny and aggravated in stretches with few islands of healthy pink tissue. I copied down her medication list, carefully spelling the unfamiliar names. Her x-rays hung in the hallway and the shadow of the knot floated in the murky abdomen.

McDermott arrived and read my chart note.

"I have two patients with Crohn's disease," she said. "I've actually learned a lot from Carla." She talked about medications she had tried and said that steroids usually helped.

"Anyway," she said, interrupting herself impatiently, "I talked to Gregg Tsai already." Dr. Tsai was a gastroenterologist from Boston who had recently finished his specialty training. He worked with McDermott in the clinic across the street, and it was easy enough to communicate about shared patients when they passed in the hallway. Tsai had recommended a novel medication that McDermott talked about for a moment. She smiled and added that Tsai wanted to place a tube to pump Carla's stomach. He wanted us to withhold food and drink for a few days of "bowel rest" and to periodically push on her belly, checking that her intestines weren't beginning to strangulate, requiring exploratory surgery.

"Good old Carla," McDermott said, chuckling. "Not certain she'll go for the tube." I wrote treatment orders and she signed below my name. We went into the room and she pressed deeply on Carla's belly. As she washed her hands briskly at the sink, she agreed that there was no immediate danger of surgery. We walked out, picked up our bags, and went to the parking lot together. I had learned that McDermott rarely lingered. She was one of two women doctors at the Missoula hospital working full time. Her schedule involved clinics, consultations on hospital patients, and inpatient call one weekend per month. Along with this schedule she juggled time with a six-year-old son and husband. I never saw her take a lunch break. When she was out of sight she was gone from the hospital grounds altogether—attending, I assumed, to everything else. For the first time I could imagine what my own life might look like one day and I found it a bit unsettling.

In the morning I ran into Gregg Tsai, who was moving somewhat rigidly as though his back bothered him. He was fuming. "She refused the tube!" he said. He shook his head a few times and I interpreted the edge in his voice to mean he was wasting his time if Carla wouldn't cooperate. Finally he talked about the novel monoclonal antibody treatment he'd recommended and calmed down.

In the hospital room Carla was staring ahead with her arms

crossed and a pouty curl on her mouth. She had just showered. Her wet blond hair was combed down neatly and hung
close to her head, and she looked like a housecat after a bath.

"You don't look too happy," I said.

"I just met Dr. Tsai," she said sharply.

"So did I."

"He wanted to put down the tube."

I said, "Why did he do that?"

"Because I'm still vomiting."

"Are you still vomiting?"

"Yes." She glanced over to the window.

"But you refused."

She sighed. "Well, he said if I'm vomiting tomorrow he'll
put it down no matter what."

"Does that seem reasonable?"

"No."

I paused to think of another line of reasoning. Then she
said, "Whatever. Maybe if I'm not getting better."

"Well, everybody wants you to get better."

When I came back later, a tube ran in through her right
nostril, taped to her cheek. She was sitting stiffly to keep the
plastic from chafing against her throat. The canister behind
the bed contained a small amount of the bluish fluid I had
seen in the ER.

"Don't I look ridiculous?" Carla sighed. I sat down in a
chair and we exchanged a few comments about the hospital.
Then I asked how long she had suffered from Crohn's disease
and she told me a story that involved most of her young life
and small-town Montana. She had been born and raised in

Shelby, a town of five thousand close to the Canadian border, the dimpled, blond baby sister to three cheerful athletic brothers. By almost every account she had lived her teenage years enviably. She had excelled in classes and when she was named editor of the high school yearbook, students crossed cliques to curry her favor, seeking her powers as spin-doctor of memory. Only her family knew that she suffered constantly from piercing cramps and unpredictable spasms of diarrhea. She began to name for me every public toilet in Shelby and then broke off, having made her point. The ailments worsened when the family vacationed at a lake cabin high in the mountains, she said. Fast food and mountain spring water particularly aggravated the crampy diarrhea. Sometimes on those trips she developed violent bouts of vomiting. She learned to travel with bottled water and avoid greasy food.

"My brothers thought I had an eating disorder," she said. "I was always skinny, which was great."

A family doctor diagnosed a nervous stomach, sent off blood tests, and suggested pills for diarrhea and depression. The medications nauseated her and did nothing for the original problem. She asked to see the nearest gastroenterologist, who practiced one hundred miles away in Great Falls. Carla remembers the doctor saying, "The problem is in your head." He denied repeated requests for a referral.

Disenfranchised, she continued to pick at food, skip school, and spar with her mother. After graduating from high school, she went to the lake with brothers newly returned from college and one night developed what she describes as "the worst cramps of my life." Early the next morning she lay on an operating table while a surgeon removed eighteen inches of her large intestine. Beefy and red from years of inflammation, the intestine was collapsed down and attached in places. In several spots it had closed completely, blocking passage.

The eviscerated organ was passed off the surgical field and sealed in a plastic bag, carried to the laboratory, and stored in a freezer overnight. In the morning the specimen was stained purple and sliced into wafer-thin sections. A pathologist looking down into a microscope saw crypts drilled through intestinal wall and rows of cells deformed by inflammation. Without hesitating, he picked up the phone. "Crohn's disease," he told the surgeon.

"Crohn's disease," the gastroenterologist told Carla and her parents at bedside.

"There are books about this disease. There's plenty of information on the Internet," she said. After a moment she looked straight at me and said, "Why don't doctors know about this disease?"

She went home to relearn living. Crohn's called for a strict diet and multiple pills and for weeks she swung low, envisioning a lifetime's acquiescence to disease. She felt misunderstood by parents, brothers, and friends. She considered postponing college.

After weeks of deliberation, Carla moved to Missoula and enrolled in school. Freshman year was the loneliest year of her life, she said. Her new friends didn't understand the routines she kept, and she was tired of constant explanations.

"Even my boyfriend sometimes says it's just in my head," she said.

McDermott was the first doctor she liked and respected. They met not long after Carla started at the university, and Carla remembered distinctly how the busy doctor had scheduled forty-five minutes to talk and then listened quiet as a stone to her story. Later when I thought about Carla's case, I realized that McDermott was probably the first doctor to really hear her story. Now I understood why Carla wanted to sue her hometown doctor and could see why she had dueled with Tsai over the tube, having lived with much illness because of physician error.

Then Carla spoke of a cousin in Wyoming with similar cramps and diarrhea. A local doctor had advised the cousin the problem was menstrual. Carla turned to me and said assuredly, "Crohn's disease runs in families and I told her that. I told her to get another doctor and get checked."

"That's true," I said.

Carla sighed. "She won't do it. She says he's the doctor and he knows best."

Later she dropped the lawsuit after realizing she just wanted a working digestive system, which legal wrangling would never produce. Still, she was understandably horrified by the prospect that she might have suffered needlessly and that her experiences might not help anyone else.

Carla felt markedly better with three days of hospitalization and her pain was exorcised without further painkillers. After deliberating with McDermott and Tsai, I had the tube removed. Carla began to feel hungry and tentatively took bites of fruit and drank chicken soup. Before she left the hospital, we reviewed each of her medications. She explained which pills worked for what symptoms. One seemed to have no effect at all and we agreed to shelve that for the time being. We talked about the number of bathroom visits she could stand in a day and agreed on which medication she would adjust if the diarrhea worsened. Finally I sent her home with McDermott's blessing and a return clinic appointment scheduled for one month.

I would be gone to another locale by then, so I knew I would never see Carla again. When I thought about her later I marveled over how, at a young age, she had found wisdom for what her body could and couldn't do. I surveyed attending physicians about magic spells that opened patients' eyes and all replied with stories of private epiphanies that had nothing to do with doctors or hospitals or medicine. I sensed that Carla's watchfulness and deep knowledge of her disease came from years of battling disbelieving family and "experts" over her pain and stomach symptoms. I wondered who looked out for her now. I thought she trusted McDermott to look out for her, and I knew she looked out for herself. My role was to believe what she told me and act as her partner, providing her the tools to modulate Crohn's disease and smooth out the bumps so she could otherwise live the way she desired.

The final exam in internal medicine started at 8:00 A.M. in a classroom above the Missoula hospital library. The test would be a daylong grind, and immediately afterward I planned to pack my few things and leave for Spokane with Amanda, the other medical student rotating with me in Missoula. The local news channels had predicted a snowstorm for western Montana that night and we hoped to leave ahead of the treacherous weather. As we walked into the classroom I thought of fellow internal medicine students in Seattle, who would begin taking their final exam an hour after us because of the time zone difference. The test proctor passed out the tests as soon as we were sitting down. Amanda and I looked at each other, smiled, shrugged, and began reading. The morning filled up with multiple choice situations about patients withdrawing from alcohol, men and women who suffered from pneumonia or low blood counts, who might have lymphoma or sarcoidosis or scabies. I penciled my responses onto the answer sheet, trying to move at an even pace through the questions. Amanda was still writing when I handed in the first section of the test. I walked outside with a sandwich I had packed for lunch, my brain overloaded from the morning's mental exercise, and I went to eat in a corner of the hospital that looked out to the Bitterroot Mountains.

After I finished the sandwich and sat quietly for a while, I returned to the classroom. The proctor looked up from the book she was reading. She had already booted up the computers and the first screen of the afternoon's exam waited, ready. I settled in at the keyboard and typed my name and student number and suddenly I was inside a clinical adventure game. The first patient was a homeless man who arrived at the hospital coughing up green sputum. I requested a lung exam, which the computer reported as normal on the left with greatly diminished breath sounds on the right. I ordered a chest x-ray and the computer pulled up a film showing a white shadow draped across the right lung, so I asked the computer to put a needle in the fluid there.

When I'd solved that case I moved along to a middle-aged bartender who'd had difficulty breathing and sleeping. The physical exam and first series of tests indicated he had heart failure and liver disease, and I felt it a sure thing that alcohol had caused his problem, even though he denied serious consumption. Further lab results suggested something besides alcohol, but I couldn't quite name one single disease that explained all the lab abnormalities. Finally I ran out of time and diagnosed the patient with a case of alcoholic heart failure with liver congestion from fluid overload, even though it didn't seem to be the right answer. The computer whirred and blinked and a few moments later the screen flashed the answer that the patient had advanced hemochromatosis and would need his blood drawn off to reduce the iron overload. I sat back in my chair, deflated, and took a deep breath. I closed my eyes, rubbed my face, and then stretched my arms. I was not feeling like a very good doctor, and I was feeling especially ready for the test to be finished.

Finally I hit the return key. The last case was a twenty-two-year-old with a high fever and sore throat and lymph nodes. I knew I would get this case correct. Still slouched down in my seat, I typed in my differential diagnosis, ordered lab tests, checked back on the patient, made his diagnosis, arranged a follow-up appointment, and signed off.

When I walked into the apartment to pack up the few things I'd brought to Missoula, Amanda came downstairs and said, "Hemochromatosis! Can you believe that?"

"What in God's name!"

Then mercifully, she said, "Let's get out of town."

An hour later we were on the road, caravanning at thirty miles an hour in whiteout conditions and trading the lead from time to time. I felt completely drained, and I couldn't help frustrating myself with thoughts of how I was not going be a good doctor. I had assumed a reasonable man to be a heavy drinker and missed his treatable diagnosis. It didn't seem important at that moment that I'd seen a large range of disease and dug down into peoples' lives and the place where I'd lived for two months. All I thought of was how a doctor shouldn't make mistakes, even if the mistakes were paper mistakes, even if real practice allowed you references and consultants and chances for amendment.

My thoughts drifted to Velma Carter, who I had left behind to browsing deer and the Bitterroot Mountains and bemused doctors. "Crocheting is for grannies!" she had snapped, after pointing out the long years before I would be a practicing doctor, the eternity of days and nights where everything I knew and did evolved and solidified. This cheered me a bit.

We came up on Lookout Pass and eased off the highway at the Montana border. The sky had lightened and cleared on the pass and as we came out of the snowstorm I was filled with relief, as though I had survived something myself. Semi-trailer rigs lined the shoulder and their drivers were wrapping chains around tall wheels before the slide down into Idaho. We walked up the hillside above the pass and through dark evergreens to watch the comet Hale-Bopp streaking ahead of its blunt yellow tail.

I stood for a few moments taking in the awe of the night sky and warming to thoughts of home.

CHAPTER 6

Swaziland

◆◆◆◆◆◆◆◆◆◆

WWAMI had intoxicated me with the idea of medical
adventure and by the end of third year I was fanta-
sizing about taking my stethoscope beyond the rural Pacific
Northwest. My idea was to drop into the remote Third World,
which I pictured to be loud and dusty and tropical, and which
I had begun romanticizing aggressively. I thought of the trip
as a test of the doctoring skills I'd learned, and I would discover whether I connected with patients in a radically different place.

The University of Washington did not offer rotations in
Guatemala or Vietnam, like some schools, but my fourth-
year schedule was relatively open and I could arrange my own
clerkship abroad. When I returned to Seattle from Missoula,
I was directed to a binder in the Department of Family Practice office listing all of the international hospitals and clinics
where medical students had worked, which was shelved next
to black binders labeled "Alaska," "Idaho," and "Wyoming."
The big international book was arranged by continent. In all
there were probably forty contacts and I pored over descriptions of the clinics and towns, wrote a list of the most appeal-
ing, then sent missives to doctors in countries like Kenya,
Haiti, Ethiopia, and Indonesia, asking if anyone wanted an
extra pair of hands.

Replies trickled in: three hospitals were fully booked with

medical students for the coming year, one American physician had completed his Central American mission and was back to practicing in the United States, and a pair planned to go abroad the same time I was assigned to an emergency medicine rotation in Seattle. After months, a letter addressed in cramped cursive pen arrived from southern Africa. The letter was handwritten by the chief surgeon at a hospital in Swaziland, a former British colony of 1 million cradled on three sides by a South Africa throwing off apartheid, and lawless Mozambique abutting the eastern border. The hospital could take me, the surgeon wrote. Could I please reply with my travel dates? He would send a driver for me at the airport.

Viral syndrome" was the chart diagnosis.

The patient, Moses Dlamini, had been admitted early that morning to the hospital in Manzini, Swaziland, and now lay on top of the bedsheets with delirium shining in his eyes. He was skinny and sinewy and naked except for a dark print cloth covering him at the waist, and he seemed unaware of his visibly rough breathing.

A family practice resident from Oregon named Frank circled the bed, drying his hands on a towel. Frank had arrived in Swaziland a week earlier. He was tall with dark bushy hair and he wore a long white coat buttoned neatly over scrubs. He read from the chart, saying, "Basically, he's had six weeks of shortness of breath with fevers and chills. Not coughing anything up. No blood. No previous medical history."

I leaned down and felt chains of round lymph nodes under Moses' chin. His lungs crackled faintly at the top of each breath. Frank's hand crossed mine, zigzagging quickly and precisely across the bony back, and then he snapped the stethoscope into his coat pocket. I felt Moses' abdomen, which had sunken down with skin pulled tightly across, and his flesh yielded sluggishly.

"Open your mouth," Frank ordered. A nursing student named Tsembayena repeated Frank's request in Siswati, the Swazi language that sounds like Xulu. Moses continued staring distractedly out the window, and I moved to open his jaw for him. His tongue was covered with a thick white carpet.

"Looks like thrush," I said, scraping his tongue with a wooden blade. Thrush is a fungal infection common in HIV. Frank raised an eyebrow. The lymph nodes and thrush pointed to advanced HIV, and I didn't understand why the chart had labeled his disease a viral syndrome. Being unfamiliar with local convention, though, I didn't want to air the ambiguity to the delirious patient and his neighbors. I turned to Frank and said, "Should we test him?"

"The test doesn't arrive until next week."

"Is that what they do?"

"I think they try to test," Frank said.

"He seems really tired."

"No, he doesn't look good."

"What about a chest x-ray?"

A nurse in a powder blue nursing pinafore pulled a chest x-ray from his folder and we looked carefully with bright sunshine coming from behind the image. Both lung fields showed a fine, lacy pattern. I crossed my arms and scrutinized Moses again, longing for him to tell his story. I had never taken care of a patient with AIDS and I couldn't tell from the examination whether he had one of the rare infections that only strikes AIDS patients or a more common affliction like Streptococcal pneumonia. It was possible that his acute illness was actually progression of the HIV and not a superimposed infection, and there was a chance he didn't have HIV after all but something entirely different.

Finally I said, "That x-ray could be Pneumocystis."

"We can't test for that here."

"You can't test for much here."

"True."

"We should probably just start Bactrim, don't you think? Do you have Bactrim?" American HIV patients received this drug to prevent Pneumocystis pneumonia once the T-cell count dropped low enough. Patients who weren't protected commonly developed this serious pneumonia, which became rapidly fatal when untreated.

Frank turned to the nurse. "Let's give a dose of Bactrim now, please, and oxygen by nasal cannula." I scribbled the prescription on an order sheet. Moses looked away from us.

"Is the attending going to round with us?" I said.

Frank paused and said, "He's gone home to Zaire for a funeral." Zaire was a thousand miles away. "I hear he gets back later this week."

"Because Moses looks sick."

"Yes, an attending would be great," Frank said. Then he pointed me toward a patient in the next bed and crossed the ward to begin on a third patient. I knew we had a busy clinic waiting as soon as we finished rounds but I was dismayed to see him move off so quickly. We had no answers for Moses and a plan that seemed unlikely to improve his condition. Now I understood that day one in sub-Saharan Africa would be a junior resident and me caring for dozens of sick men at the old mission, and I understood that the basic goal was to keep people alive. I turned my back to Moses and meekly approached the second bed, digesting a short chart note attesting to acute malaria. The patient spoke with the whirs and clicks of the Swazi language and Tsembayena translated that the patient's headache had improved after he received an intravenous antimalarial drug. I leaned down to touch him with my stethoscope, slowly formulating a plan as I listened. Then I turned to Frank and reported what I'd seen. I suggested a switch from the intravenous medication to antimalarial pills, and Frank waved me on.

"Fine. You don't have to ask unless you have a question." He spun off toward yet another patient down the line of beds. Watching him hop from bed to bed I felt slow and ungainly. I was full of questions about the two patients I'd seen and the diseases I had only read about and memorized for multiple-choice tests. There would be no wise sage to guide me this time in the ways of disease and suffering; this time I would have to rely on the compass I carried inside.

I wrote a short chart note and gave orders to the nurse, feeling something descend over me.

My clinic was the fourth door down one of the mission's airy hallways and opened up to a spacious cloister. The clinic room was a basic cement cell painted the color of limes with ceilings rising twenty feet up and dirty light filtering through a small glass portal just beneath the ceiling. The air stayed cool and slightly damp inside, a relief from the relentless dry heat. Three other adult medicine clinic rooms along the same hallway were variably open for business. Outside, patients sat pressed together on benches around the perimeter, waiting to see a doctor.

I had not been in the room three minutes, pushing the exam table against the wall and repositioning the desk, when a young man named Khosi burst through the door mumbling a greeting. Later I learned that patients watched vigilantly for doctors and if you did not call for a patient shortly, someone inevitably knocked. Now Khosi walked to the exam table with great haste, unbuckled his belt, and reached into his shorts. Glancing his way, I saw that his penis had eroded into a bloody mess.

"What is this, madam?" he demanded. His English was fluent and proper. I pulled on latex gloves. After wiping away blood and congealed white material, I saw a circular ulcer eating into the skin. He stared incredulously at the lesion, unable to shift his eyes.

"When did this happen?"

"Last week."

"Had anything like it before?"

"No," he said. He turned his head and exhaled loudly as I touched a chain of painful lymph nodes tunneling through his groin. I glanced at his medical card, which showed a blood test result from earlier that morning.

"Listen, I think this is syphilis," I said, pleased that the diagnosis had fallen together. I took the gloves off, washed my hands, and went through the curtain looking for an attending doctor to confirm his story. The adjoining rooms were empty and I continued down the hall to the emergency room, where there was still no sign of an attending. A nursing student said everyone had gone for morning tea. I turned back to my clinic room, past fifteen patients waiting in the cloister, and sat at my desk copying the treatment for syphilis from a manual.

Presently I glanced at Khosi leaning against the table with arms crossed and head tipped sharply. He took the prescription from me and strolled away coolly. I trailed him out, closed the door behind him, and sat down to read about syphilis. The disease rarely occurred in the United States anymore except in urban pockets, and I'd never seen a case.

In a moment Khosi knocked at the door, looked in, and said, "Madam, the pharmacy doesn't have the medication."

I took the prescription from him, went out to the cloister, and cut to the front of the pharmacy line waving the card.

"You don't have penicillin?" I said.

"Yes. Sorry," the pharmacist said sympathetically, rolling the r's in "sorry," his English tempered with the whirs and clicks of Siswati. He slid open the glass window and leaned out toward me. He was wearing a thin button-down shirt and a slim blue cloth tie and was sweating under his arms. "Sometimes we have the penicillin but not today."

"When will you have it?"

"Maybe Thursday, or next Thursday." He explained that the government sent medication shipments weekly but his requests weren't always promptly filled. He added that they had been waiting some time for the shipment, which was held up by another budget crisis.

"What do you have that's similar?"

"We have some tablets that your friend brought," he said. He handed over a bottle of pills that Frank had procured from a pharmaceutical representative in the United States. I unscrewed the lid and swirled about two dozen pills in the bottom of the bottle.

"I'll think about it," I said.

I passed Frank in front of the emergency room.

"Can I run something by you?" I said.

"Sure, of course."

"This guy has a single painless genital ulcer and he's RPR positive, so it's probably syphilis, but the pharmacy doesn't have penicillin."

"I know how that goes," he said, smiling through one corner of his mouth. "Why don't you use Augmentin and give him doxy in case he's got silent chlamydia."

"There won't be any Augmentin left after this guy." Frank had told me that he'd brought two hundred tablets of the antibiotic along with a crate of Tylenol, and most of his supply had been confiscated by Swaziland customs.

"It's all gone?" he said. After a long pause he said, "Your call," and disappeared back into his clinic.

I went back inside my exam room and crossed penicillin off Khosi's card. I tapped the pen against my temple, wondering if I should save the strong antibiotic for a severe AIDS-related infection on the ward. I couldn't imagine how I would select one patient in the throes of dying to bless with the special antibiotic, and then I would still have the problem of how to treat syphilis next time. Finally I decided to use what was left of the Augmentin and handed the revised prescription to Khosi.

When he was out the door, I remembered that I hadn't told him to use condoms, which would protect him and his partners better than any medicine a doctor could provide. I had focused so intently on his slice of story and not ventured even a step beyond to discover the lifestyle he lived or how he understood his own sexual risk. That was a kind of blindness, I suddenly remembered, and because of it I had neglected to talk about safety and monogamy and treating his partner.

An HIV test hadn't even entered my mind.

After clinic I walked rapidly down the streets into town, passing a dusty field where a soccer match was being played, and crossed a bridge where traffic rushed past at free-way speeds just a few feet away. When I reached the edge of the city proper, the streets were suddenly filled with people. Up the main road was a row of storefront buildings and a fast-food restaurant named Chicken Lickin. Many in the crowd walked at a fast clip and carried briefcases and shoulder bags. A layer of red dust covered buildings and cars and mingled damply with my skin. I turned off the main road, passed the open market where women sold maize and produce, and entered an air-conditioned supermarket that anchored a strip of textile shops, a hairdresser, and a travel agency. Sacks of ground maize sat in tall white stacks at the front of the store. I browsed cereal and bread with vaguely British packaging and gathered up rice, squash, broccoli, and chutney.

Walking home, I thought about how I had just depleted the

hospital's best antibiotics, which were no longer available to the sicker patient who might roll into the emergency room tonight or be admitted tomorrow. I was mad that I'd had to help one individual at another's expense. Then I thought about HIV patients on the ward. Those with full-blown AIDS were easy to spot, with lymph nodes embedded just below the skin, and thrush adherent to tongues, and I'd intuited that these patients were beyond recovery. It had just occurred to me that some of the healthy-looking patients in clinic harbored early HIV, and that all of the uninfected were at risk. In a state of limited resources, a doctor might have to choose who to help and who to abandon. The calculus was akin to wartime triage, where the mortally wounded were the lowest priority. The choice seemed straightforward: you helped those who had a chance to survive. But touching the sickest patients on the ward every morning blurred that calculus. Now I climbed the mission steps with groceries weighing heavily on my arms.

L ater that week a teenager named Sibusisso was waiting in the clinic when I arrived from ward rounds. His hair was shaved down to curly stubble and he had long bony limbs. He said, "Madam, it hurts when I pee." I was hearing this complaint from two or three patients each day and felt a cheerful ripple of confidence knowing I had a drug formula to use on him. I sat at the desk and asked the usual litany of questions, stood to examine the area in question, and then said, "You most likely have gonorrhea."

I sat again and rapidly wrote out a three-drug formula that

accounted for the pharmacy's limited antibiotic choices and would treat both gonorrhea and chlamydia. Initially I had some disaffection for the cocktail, knowing it was difficult to take two weeks of medication, three times daily, especially when one upset your stomach. In the United States, I knew doctors gave two pills and a shot in the arm right in clinic and the infections would be fully treated, with no chance of drug resistance in patients who didn't finish the medications. But I was glad to offer anything at all.

Sibusisso eyed me.

"How did I get this gonorrhea?" he asked.

"You got it from sex," I said.

"What?" he said, blushing.

"People catch gonorrhea from sex," I said. "The antibiotics will cure you if you take all of the pills."

After a time he said, "I shouldn't sleep with any women while I'm taking the medication."

"No, wait until you're finished with the pills."

Sibusisso pressed his lips together.

I said, "Tell me this. Do you use condoms?"

"No."

"You will catch this disease again unless you use a condom every time you have sex."

"I didn't know," he said.

"Women can catch this disease from you right now," I said. I handed him the medical card.

"Please use condoms," I said.

"Thank you very much," he said.

When he left, I shut the door before another patient could

slip in. I was horrified and bewildered now that I could see the emerging story. I'd wrongly assumed so much and now understood that maybe none of my patients connected their diseases with sex and none were regularly using condoms.

I stood in the middle of the exam room thinking of patients whose diseases had temporarily abated with my antibiotics. Those men had likely resumed unprotected sex and were spreading disease flagrantly again, I realized. All the hard work of the first week had brought just the briefest respite. To make my doctoring go further, I would have to preach condom use knowing that a single condom was as expensive as a doctor's visit plus a course of antibiotics, which cost sixty cents. I would plug for monogamy, knowing that multiple wives still attested to a man's power.

I paced the room, thinking incredulously of how 40 percent of the population was infected with HIV and the life expectancy had collapsed to thirty-nine years. I could just about flip a coin to determine if Sibusisso was infected with HIV. The epidemic raged on, and yet there was deep silence in public and private discourse as entire homesteads and towns were devoured.

Now I resolved to make a leap and offer HIV testing to all of my patients. I would be blunt, and I would answer to my conscience.

The attending doctor Akintayo appeared on the medical ward one morning after Frank and I had begun our rounds. Akintayo was a tall, heavy man with thick glasses and an ironic grin, and he wore an immaculately pressed white coat. He had just returned from a funeral in Zaire. Several years ago the Zairean government had sent him to Swaziland as an offering of humanitarian aid, a typical route doctors followed to the hospital in Manzini. In fact, all of the attending doctors originated from one of the richer and more influential African countries like Zaire or Ethiopia or Uganda, all except Bahoyo, who was on loan from the Philippines for two years. Most thought of their work as a calling, whether humanitarian or religious, and this idea was reinforced by scanty and often delayed pay. Several doctors considered themselves Christian missionaries even though the hospital's formal ties with any church had ended ten years earlier, due to lack of converts. Akintayo, like most of his colleagues, lived in a modest single-story house on the mission compound. He had brought his wife, two beautiful teenage daughters, and a young son with him from Zaire. He did not own the house or even have a car, but he had been able to send his eldest son away to college in Kenya.

Now we all congregated at Moses' bedside, reviewing the presumptive viral diagnosis and treatment we had started.

"Oh yes," Akintayo said, grinning. "Undoubtedly that is the diagnosis." He added that they had no way to test for Pneumocystis pneumonia at the hospital, but he liked for treatment to account for the possibility.

Today, Moses looked substantially brighter. He was sitting alertly at the edge of the bed, hot and trembling, but breathing calmly. Oxygen had never been given. I rewrote the order in the chart, underlining emphatically.

"Could you get oxygen for Mr. Dlamini?" Frank said, turning

to face the nurse behind him. The nurse nodded vigorously, her hands clasped together over a pale blue nursing pinafore.

"The rapid antibody test has come," Akintayo said. "It arrived yesterday." He pointed to a man with a long laboratory coat drawing the morning's blood tests on the ward.

"You," Akintayo said, and his grin vanished. The lab man looked up, alarmed.

"You test this man for HIV," Akintayo ordered. He pointed to Moses, then spun in a circle and pointed with bravado to four other men in the cluster of eight beds.

"I want all these men tested!"

The lab man finished drawing blood and cleaned the patient's arm, then waved his hands and backed into the vestibule. The patients' faces remained hard and distant.

"You test them!" Akintayo said.

I was in the emergency room listening to a much-anticipated radio speech by the Swazi king, then jumped up suddenly and went searching anxiously about the hospital for someone to talk with. Frank was taking morning tea in the cafeteria. I watched him butter his toast rapidly. I must have looked a little stunned because after a moment he said, "Can I get you a drink?" I nodded and he popped up, waved a hand across the counter, and walked back pushing the steaming mug toward me.

"Did you hear the king's address?" I said.

Frank's face turned contemptuous. He said, "That was the lamest thing I've ever heard." He took a long swallow of hot tea, then chewed off a bite of toast.

"You know what they say," I said, glancing around. "People are very critical that he's taken so few wives." Nursing students had passed on this bit of gossip. Then something clicked. The king was twenty-eight years old. He had acquired four wives and from the wives had nine children in one decade of his rule. His father, the previous king, had left dozens of wives and three hundred children. Condoms prevented men from carrying out God's work, King Mswati had exclaimed joyfully over the airwaves. Go forth and multiply.

When I looked up, the expression on Frank's face had changed. He turned his words over before he said, "Listen, I tested a woman this morning just for the hell of it. I don't know what made me think it. Nice, normal lady. She was positive."

"How old?"

"Twenty-nine." Anger surged in me.

"Did you tell her?"

"Not yet."

"You better tell her."

"I will," he said.

"Although I heard people commit suicide if they learn they're HIV-positive," I said. A translator had told me this when I'd suggested HIV testing to a patient that morning. I had shyly started asking all of my patients to get tested and many had agreed, then never arrived in the laboratory to have the test drawn. I felt I was getting the message out, though, that anybody was at risk, and I was beginning to feel it wrong not to mention HIV to patients.

"Is that true?"

"I asked the nurses and they thought so."

"That complicates it," he said. Here was the moral calculus again, I thought. If the doctor didn't test because of threats of patient suicide, infected patients would continue to spread HIV. The choice was between one death and many. I could not see that antiretroviral medication, which could drive the virus into quiescence, would change the calculus if it ever became affordable in Swaziland.

"Yes, but there's a consensus," I said. Bahoyo, the internist on loan from the Philippines, had said, "The test isn't totally accurate, but it's the best we have. Test them while you can." Bahoyo was petite with a freckled face and she worked with a stodgy energy. She had been away from her home and her husband and children for more than a year.

"No doubt Akintayo thinks so. I like that guy. I think he's good. But what do you do with a positive result?"

I knew he was speaking rhetorically but I couldn't help answering. "We can tell them to stop sleeping around. Tell them to use condoms," I said.

Frank looked sorrowful. "Yes. That's about all we can do."

In the next day's edition of *Swazi News*, Health Minister Dr. Phindile Dlamini defended the king's official position on HIV, which called for condom use. She declared, furthermore, that his views on procreation and HIV were in no way contradictory.

When I entered the cafeteria, someone waved from the far corner. I waved back, took a tray from the counter, and crossed the room. The waving hand was Tsembayena, the nursing student who often volunteered to help translate for patients who spoke Siswati only. Tsem was twenty years old with high cheekbones and glowing skin. She had nine months left in the nursing program and as yet no work plans for after graduation.

"Can I eat with you?" I said.

"Please," she urged, gesturing at the seat next to her.

I placed my tray on the table and saw the other nursing students' eyes drift across the beef chunks in thick colorless sauce poured over rice and fading broccoli. I had eaten the bland meal several times before and could never finish it.

"You ate something different," I said.

"We students don't get meat," she said. "Only doctors get meat."

"That doesn't make sense. I'm just a student too," I said. The table fell quiet and nobody looked at me, so I refrained from saying anything further.

I'd become quite fond of Tsem, who really seemed to enjoy being on the ward and in the clinic. I had learned that her family lived on a rural homestead about twenty kilometers up the road from Manzini to Mbabane, not far from Lozitha, the royal community. She was the second of four sisters and had one younger brother. She had mentioned that the king was a relative, and I later learned he was her uncle. Her father was a lieutenant colonel in the military. I surmised that she belonged to an elite social class, but like all of the nursing students, she slept in a mission dormitory with cracked plaster walls.

After her classmates finished eating and left for afternoon

assignments, Tsem said, "My sister has a problem on her foot. It has been bothering her for many months. Can you come to see it?"

I said I would be happy to visit but reiterated that I was a medical student and shouldn't write prescriptions, even though I had been doing just that in the mission clinic and wards. I asked if the family doctor had treated her. Previously Tsem had mentioned that her family received medical care from the Defense Department clinics, where the king went.

"It would be better if you were her doctor," Tsem said. The sister was sixteen years old and went to boarding school in Piggs Peak, in the northern hilly part of the country.

I said, "I'm off this Saturday."

Tsem's brother picked us up at the mission gate on Saturday morning and drove us in a small rattling pickup truck past the capital city, Mbabane on the high veld, and through the town of Ngwenya up winding roads into the green hills. Tsem's older sister, a college student and activist, had come along for the ride and entertained us with descriptions of clashes with the monarchy over legal polygamy and the purchase of wives, which she and her fellow students sought to outlaw forever. She said women had no legal right to own property but there had been encouraging talks with the government. I surveyed the rolling green terrain as she talked, thinking of how few women patients I'd seen in the clinic and wondering if that had any significance. Finally we arrived, parked in front of the school, and extricated ourselves from the small vehicle. The air felt warm and thin. I removed the stethoscope from my bag. Tsem led us around the main building and up a gravel road toward the dormitories. Her sister Khetsiwe came bounding down the stairs, smiling broadly when she caught our eye, and ran across the grassy yard to meet us. She asked breathlessly if I'd found the drive pretty, how I enjoyed Swaziland, and whether I planned to move there.

"You're so kind to visit all the way out here," Khetsiwe said. She shepherded us enthusiastically around the school grounds, pointing out her classrooms and the library where she studied. The edge of the grounds sloped down to a grassy valley that dropped slowly out of sight. We circled back to the dormitory and sat while Khetsiwe rolled up her pants to show me the problem leg, which was red just above the ankle with tiny pinpoint scabs. She said she'd had it for months and wondered if it was related to showering in the girls' bathroom. She'd had no fevers or other symptoms, and the leg wasn't really painful. I removed her sandals and saw she had normal feet.

"This looks like folliculitis," I said. "A skin infection."

"What can be done?" Tsem asked. She wore a concerned expression.

"It's not serious. We should have the right medicine in the hospital pharmacy," I said.

"I can send it out!" Tsem exclaimed, beaming.

Khetsiwe sighed and nodded. "Thank you, doctor," she said. I caught myself before I said, "I'm not a doctor yet."

Philomele had been ill for one month, Roger said. Roger was thickly bearded, wore tire tread sandals, and launched into Philomele's story in a deep jovial voice. At first he thought she suffered from a female condition. When she did not recover as quickly as expected, he sent her to the village healer and she won a brief respite, but the ailments returned. She had not traveled to Mozambique or anywhere on the low veld where malaria arose, he said. Now I noticed the purple scarf wrapped over her hair attesting to her status as a married woman. They had traveled from their rural village near the South African border.

"Will you detain her here in the hospital?" Roger asked. Philomele gazed up with wide round eyes. She looked twenty years younger than him and I guessed she wasn't his first wife. She breathed rapidly with a phlegmatic rumble coming from deep in her chest. Under her chin I could see the clusters of lymph nodes. Her medical card noted a moderate fever and a heart rate of 122.

I faced Roger again. He sat at the edge of the chair, his fingers fiddling with a walking stick.

"Probably so," I said finally. Philomele's expression remained static as Roger leapt up and shook my hand vigorously. He said he hoped to arrive home by dark, then bustled out and I stood to shut the door behind him. Philomele's eyes followed me from across the room.

I sat down and said, "Let's start from the beginning. What bothers you most?"

Philomele blinked. "There's blood when I go," she said.

"To the bathroom?"

"Yes."

"How much blood?"

She looked at me, puzzled.

I said, "Have you had fevers?"

"Yes."

"Sweats or chills?"

"Both."

"Vomiting?"

"No."

"Diarrhea?"

"Yes."

"Pain?"

She indicated her lower abdomen.

"Trouble breathing?"

"Yes."

"Cough up any blood?"

"No."

"Alright," I said.

On my examination, her lungs crackled loudly and I felt her heart pounding rapidly beneath her ribcage. Her stomach yielded two lumps that bobbed beneath my fingers. When I pressed deeply, she calmly reported that her abdomen hurt.

"I wonder if you have tuberculosis," I said.

"It was going around the village," she said. "I was worried."

"Let's get an x-ray and some blood tests." I scribbled her history and exam results on the medical card, then looked up and said, "I would also like to give you an HIV test."

The story was falling together in my mind now. For weeks I had been squaring off with moments of disease like an overwhelming diarrhea, a genital ulcer, and the prostration of malaria, all viewed through a veil of HIV. My questions became more precise and gradually I could imagine what patients didn't say. Human lives slowly emerged from the illness sequences in the same way I'd discovered in wwami-land. I thought again about Tsem's sister describing the low position of women in Swaziland society and tried to imagine how Philomele lived. The story was bleaker than anything I'd seen with my own eyes before. Philomele was vulnerable to tuberculosis and HIV and then to condemnation and abandonment at the hands of her own family, and she patiently accepted this as her lot.

"I think the test would be a good idea," she said pleasantly. She sat up and pulled a blanket around her shoulders and became a small, lithe face in a pile of bright cloth. We walked out to the cloister together, where the light had turned dusky and the sky was blue going purple.

"When you're done bring the films and everything to the emergency room," I said. "I'll wait for you there."

Akintayo was at work in the emergency room. He had shed his white coat for a polo shirt and jeans and he was looking after four patients at once. I went to the small desk behind the patient area and wrote Philomele's hospital orders. After a while Akintayo stuck his head in the cubby window, holding Philomele's x-rays.

"You know this woman?" he asked, pointing at the films.

I described the bloody stools and the painful abdominal lumps. "In the States we think of infections or ulcerative colitis and Crohn's," I said.

"We don't have inflammatory bowel diseases in Africa. We have tuberculosis."

"Yeah, that's what I think it is," I said.

Akintayo hung the chest x-ray, which showed infiltrates in both upper lung fields.

"What's her lymphocyte count?" Akintayo said.

I glanced down at her laboratory results and saw the lympho-cytes were abnormally high, further evidence for tuberculosis.

Akintayo turned to Philomele. "Lady, cover your mouth when you cough," he said sternly.

I went out of the emergency room with Philomele and we sat on the dark empty benches outside my clinic door.

"This is tuberculosis. That's why you're coughing and your stomach hurts. The nurse will give you your first doses of anti-biotics tonight. We'll test the stuff you're coughing up to show that it's tuberculosis. You'll have to take many months of anti-biotics to treat your illness."

"What about . . . "

"Right," I said, glancing down automatically and read, "The HIV test was negative. You don't have HIV."

I reread the unexpected result. I was learning how tubercu-losis often mingled with HIV, and Roger's willingness to shed her at the hospital, knowing something perhaps that she did not, had ignited my suspicions. I was greatly relieved to have the negative result, confident now that she would respond to our antibiotics, that her recovery would not sputter because of a rampant virus. Philomele smiled gratefully and I understood that the results conferred a certain protection in her world, where she was always at risk.

I'll be damned," Frank said. We were standing at Moses' bed-side. Moses had been walking up and down the ward with his walking stick. Frank was reading from a translucent slip of paper on the front of the chart.

"He's coughing up acid-fast bacilli."

Automatically I covered my mouth with my hand. Moses looked from me to Frank and back.

"Sorry, buddy," Frank said. "We're going to move you to the TB ward." I pointed to a room adjacent the main ward.

"What?" Moses said.

"You have tuberculosis," I said.

"The HIV test never got done," Frank said.

"We should ask again," I said.

A cheerful sense of progress pervaded the children's ward, which was located some distance from the adult male and female wards in back of the mission. In the morning, the light in the children's ward was watery and cool coming through windows that stretched up to the high ceilings. After the attending doctors Belete and Mikibi arrived, a nurse pushed an old metal cart with patient charts and medical supplies into the long tall room and nursing students trickled in after the cart. Everyone gathered around the infants, and a nursing student began to sing a Siswati hymn with her strong, clear, high voice. As she dropped into the melody the voices of nurses and mothers and doctors entered the song sounding through the cool ward. When the hymn ended, the crisp sound died slowly into the air, and then the nursing student murmured a prayer for cures and miracles.

We began rounds on the infant ward, where two rectangular stickers affixed to a glass wall read "BREAST IS BEST! Bottle feeding can kill an infant." The ward provided continuous living advertising to match the slogan. Infants slept on a wooden platform that ran the length of the room and was sep-arated into shallow two-by-four-foot beds. Mothers sat behind the platform and breastfed infants around the clock. Between nighttime feedings, the mothers moved to benches pushed against the periphery of the ward or slept on the floor. Translu-cent bags of fluid and antibiotics hung from a metal bar above the platform and ran into tiny veins through intravenous tub-ing and lines. We moved quickly through the infant patients, who suffered primarily from stomach or lung infections, and on to the toddlers next door, who lived between painted walls of knobby trees and giraffes against blue sky.

Now a boy chewing a handful of maize looked at us with an expression of gloomy concern. He was a four-year-old named Nkosi who had been abandoned by his mother because of his persistent infections, which I'd learned was sometimes the practice among impoverished families. As we approached, he leaned away from the garrulous Ugandan Mikibi, who had admitted him from the clinic the day before. Mikibi called the child a "frozen boy" and described how he only moved when absolutely necessary, grimacing and never crying out. In the clinic, he weighed in at twenty pounds—about the size of a one-year-old baby. Dark rings marking his hands and forearms proved to be abscesses in different stages of blossom, several fresh and plump and many old and fading and scarred. Mikibi had gone after the new abscesses with a long thin needle, drawing out thick rich liquid.

I swooped down with my stethoscope and Nkosi twisted away. I put a hand gently against his back and after a few moments tried again with the stethoscope. He tilted his head and frowned balefully but this time allowed me to listen, as though he understood the necessity of things being done to him. Then Mikibi wrapped a hand around Nkosi's wrist and pressed a finger to his arms and in the hollows of joints, feeling for new abscesses. He pushed on a spongy spot at the crown of Nkosi's head and suddenly Nkosi began to look very sad, remembering what had happened before and thinking of what might be coming.

"I got the big ones," Mikibi said. He regarded Nkosi. "That could become one on the back of his head. But this poor child. He's finally getting antibiotics."

Mikibi squeezed Nkosi's puffy wrists again, then turned to me and said, "Of course his big problem is kwash." He meant kwashiorkor, which is protein-deficiency malnutrition. Mikibi pointed to Nkosi's rounded stomach, where low-protein fluid pooled, as evidence of advanced kwash. The abscess wounds could take months to heal because of his poor nutritional status, and Mikibi said that gaining weight was as important as the antibiotics we provided. Nkosi had been staring at the ground and tilted his head toward me now, and I had the sobering thought that perhaps he could feel he was slowly dying. It was not, as I was learning, a terribly unusual achievement in this place, even for a four-year-old child.

The telephone rang several times before I understood that someone was calling and I remembered I was taking calls for pediatrics. The phone rang twice more while I reached down in the dark looking for the receiver. A voice said, "Please come—a child is critically ill."

I sat straight up to wake myself a little bit. I had been sleep-ing soundly under an open window and my skin was damp in the hot night air.

"Wait a minute," I said, hearing my voice come thickly off my tongue. "What's going on?"

"We have a child critically ill."

"Is he breathing?" I said.

"She is critically ill," the voice implored. "Please come right away."

"Fine, I'll be right over."

I put the phone down and leaned forward to switch on a light. The clock read ten minutes to three. I rubbed my face a few times trying to get my bearings and when I stood up I felt all of the blood draining out of my head. Then I put on run-ning shoes and a sweatshirt.

I jogged down the stairs and past the emergency room. Bahoyo's voice floated from the open door, scolding a patient. In the cloister stray cats napped on the grass. The door to the pediatrics ward was open. The hallway stunk with the acrid smell of cleaning solutions and I thought reflexively of cadaver lab as I ran through the vestibule. The lights had been dimmed on the ward. A mother fed her baby from a long breast draped down over the front of her shirt. The rest of the infants slept quietly on the platform.

"Sis." A nurse touched my arm from behind. "The other way." She pointed two doors back down into the vestibule.

In the room, two stout women stood beside the bed. Each wore a head scarf. One looked searchingly at me and the other gazed vacantly into the hallway. A shrunken four-month-old baby girl lay on the bed, her eyes flung open and lips blue. I moved her heavy chin to feel for a pulse: nothing. I leaned down with my stethoscope and listening for a long moment, heard just the hiss of oxygen blowing at her nostrils. Finally I looked at the nurse standing in the doorway.

"Do we have atropine?" I asked.

"No."

"Epinephrine?"

"Yes, but there is a problem." She pointed at the baby's head.

The head was immense. Her skin looked fragile as parchment and was pulled tightly between the fontanelles and seams of her skull like the creases of a desert floor. Her hands and arms had shriveled and wrinkly skin hung off the bone. The shine in her eyes had hardened and solidified like doll's eyes, and I saw her pupils were black and wide and stopped in time. But I still didn't believe that she had died; the nurse's phrase "critically ill" rang through my head.

The nurse said, "The IV is gone."

The IV was lying in a careless patch of clear tape alongside the baby, a few curly black hairs trapped on the tape. Sweat had probably loosened the tape from her skin and the IV had slipped out with the tape. There was no way to give a last-ditch medication to save her now. I stepped back in abject horror and then ran from the room to the nursing station and telephoned the switchboard for Belete, the attending backup. The switchboard phone rang twenty times without an answer and finally I hung up. I ran into the janitorial closet next door and dry heaved over the sink. In the hall I told the nurse to telephone

Belete. I deliberately looked away from the baby's room so I would not see the infant's hard stillness. Then I ran for the emergency room to catch Bahoyo. When I arrived, breathless and dizzy, the emergency room was empty of patients and two nurses sat in chairs talking. I rushed into the room.

"Where is Bahoyo?" I demanded.

"She went home."

"Where is Belete?"

"Belete hasn't been here," the nurse said. "What happened?"

"One of the infants on the pediatric ward was . . . " I said.

"Very ill?" the nurse said.

"No," I said. "She wasn't . . . anything . . . when I got there."

The nurse was suddenly standing and folding me down into her chair. She watched me breathe in great gasps.

"Shame, sis," she said. She knelt next to me and smoothed my hair with her broad hand. "Shame. It happens sometimes. It does. Sorry. Sorry." She rolled the r's in "sorry" like a dirge.

After a while I said, "Will you call the pediatrics ward and ask them to turn off the oxygen?"

From the phone she said, "Do you want to pronounce?"

I looked at her.

She turned back to the phone and said, "You will have to do that."

I went into the cloister now and watched the cats sleeping on the grass. One woke, yawned, rolled over, fell to her other side, and dropped back to sleep. Then I went slowly up the stairs and into the apartment. The flicker and hum of the kitchen lights seemed terribly lonely when I came in. From the kitchen I could see the bed in disarray, where I had leapt from the sheets in haste. I crawled through the kitchen window and sat on the roof, holding my knees close to my chest, and gazed over the cloister. A sickle-shaped moon dropped slowly through the night sky. In the distance the air above Manzini was orange and pink. For some time I looked at my dark clinic door, shadowy under the eaves. Behind the mission a rooster began to crow. When I finally felt tired, I crawled back into the apartment and slept restlessly for two hours until bright sunshine woke me.

In the morning I found Belete in the nursery and he glanced up immediately. I didn't know what he had heard about the baby girl dying and now I felt embarrassed about my dramatic reaction.

He folded the stethoscope into his pocket and said, "I'm sorry about the girl."

"I tried to reach you," I said. Hastily I explained how the infant was no longer breathing by the time I'd arrived, that I'd asked for epinephrine and atropine and discovered that her IV had fallen out. Belete shook his head sympathetically.

"That girl, there was not much," he said, gesturing with his hands. "She was very far gone when she came to the hospital. You will find them like that sometimes. The infants with diarrhea can be like that."

"But we can treat diarrhea," I said. "That should pass in a few days."

"Was the mother there?" Belete said.

"There were two women. Why?"

"If the mother isn't there it should give you an idea," he said. He walked around and steered me outside to the bright breezy doorway away from the new mothers nursing babies.

When we could talk privately he said, "Sometimes the diarrhea never goes away because the babies have HIV. They seem healthy for one month or maybe two. Then they get watery diarrhea."

"That baby had HIV?" I said.

He nodded vigorously. "Oh, yes. She was here twice before but never got better."

He saw the look on my face and said, "There is nothing you can do. I'm sorry."

"Are you sure she had HIV?"

"If the mother has died, you can be almost certain the infant has HIV."

"Do you ever test the babies?"

"No."

"Do you test the mothers?"

"We don't see the mothers."

He turned and began walking back to the nursery. I stood in the sunny doorway, astonished by this last cruel twist. Who would remember this child if the mother was dead, or dying? I knew that the attending doctors forgot quickly, having looked after scores of similar patients. I wondered if I would forget too by week's end, when fresh tragedies replaced this one. Now a fuzzy sensation fell over me, as though I had heard of her dying on the television news, and I turned away from the nursery.

For a time everything became distant. I didn't feel particularly blue, just a certain vague disconnection. I herded patients through clinic, recorded their illnesses on their medical cards, and sent them away with paracetamol or diphenhydramine, over-the-counter medications to soothe fever, aches, runny nose, and nausea. In the mornings I jolted awake at dawn and couldn't fall back to sleep, and finally I'd roll out of bed feeling flat and dull. After ward rounds I took a long tea in the cafeteria while patients waited in the choking cloister, and I contemplated an early exit from Swaziland to meet up with an old friend who had moved to Spain. My days felt like sleepwalking.

About that time I accidentally stuck myself in the left hand with a needle I'd used to drain the abdominal fluid of a young man with giant clusters of lymph nodes that sprouted beneath his chin and underarms and pushed his abdomen out. When I realized what I'd done, I dropped the needle and syringe into a round metal bowl, ran to the nurse's sink, and scrubbed frantically with hot water and antiseptic soap. We could not name or treat his disease and for all I knew, he had end-stage AIDS. I had undertaken the procedure only to alleviate his discomfort, and I flogged myself with the question, as I swallowed AZT and protease inhibitors to prevent HIV infection, of whether the suffering I had temporarily alleviated had been worth the personal risk.

Eventually I vowed to carry on, and I decided to remain in Swaziland for the duration of the term I'd volunteered to work. Gradually I realized that the burden of disease and death at the hospital had finally overwhelmed me. I felt like I lived in an awake paralysis. Later I came to believe that the choice to continue working called on something fundamental to being a doctor, which is that a doctor works because there is suffering and because he or she is able. For a time in Africa I could not muster compassion and grief for every suffering human. I convinced myself that to feel and to act could be entirely unrelated things, but I decided that a doctor who sees suffering must act, rejecting the choice of not acting, even when futility and risk run high.

So every morning I put on my long skirt and white coat, gathered up reference handbooks and stethoscope, and walked downstairs into the cloister to face the day's patients.

One evening I began my call shift in the emergency room taking care of a nine-year-old with asthma who had run out of medication, a baby with diarrhea, a teenager with stomach pain. After tying up the cases, I went upstairs to the medical student apartment to fix dinner. I kept awake reading for a few hours, knowing that most calls would come before midnight. Finally I lay down when I felt my body turn achy. The phone rang at two in the morning while I was sleeping lightly in the warm air.

"We have a patient for you," the emergency room nurse said. She provided a few details about an infant with two days of gastroenteritis and I slid out of bed thinking of how quickly I could package up the case. In fifteen minutes I could see the kid, start IV fluids, and order antibiotics if he seemed sick. I still might not be fully awake by the time I finished and could just fall back into bed. When I stood, the room spun a few times slowly, then settled down.

When I came into the ER, the nurse Patricia pointed me to the patient's gurney and the mother leaned against the wall watching me with a cryptic expression. Underneath the blanket, the infant looked like a ghost in an enormous diaper, just bones and loose skin. His chest heaved grimly for air. I touched his rough desiccated tongue, listened to his chest, felt his boggy belly, and squeezed the skin hanging from his arms. His eyes were bright and sunk deeply in the sockets.

"You've got to get a line in him," I said to Patricia. I scratched out admission orders quickly while Patricia worked on his veins. Shortly she looked over and said, "I've had no luck." I picked up the phone and called Belete to come in immediately. I felt over the infant's body for a candidate vein and began to realize I knew how the story would proceed.

Belete arrived and pointed the surgical lamp at the infant's neck. "I've never seen anything like this," he said. He searched for the blue of the jugular, then began threading needle catheters into anything along the skull that hinted at being a vessel. The infant vomited a little bit of milk. Belete turned the infant's head to keep him from swallowing the vomit and choking but his breathing had already started to slow. A catheter flapped impotently from his skull. The infant vomited soundlessly again and after a few moments he was no longer breathing. Belete looked at me, then sat down in back of the ER. I did not move, watching the infant's chest desperately for a breath, incredulous over how fast he had spiraled away. I placed my hands on the table. Then I became aware of the mother standing beside me and when I turned, her eyes were like stones.

"I'm sorry," I said. Her face crumpled and I reached

automatically for her. I stood rubbing her back while she shook with great loud sobs and I held her until she was no longer shaking. Then the mother's companions came to her and, taking her arms, walked her outside. She hiccuped with grief and began to wail disconsolately again as the women engulfed her going out the door. I watched her walk out, then I left through the front door and walked up to my flat. As soon as I was inside I got into bed, pulled the bedcovers over my head, and let everything flow over me, as though I lay at the bottom of a river.

In the morning I dressed for work and folded the stethoscope into a pocket of my white coat. I left the treatment manuals sitting on the bedroom desk and went downstairs into the crisp sunny morning. The white coat felt so light on my shoulders without the chunky reference books that I practically felt like I was floating. Now I turned down the footpath to the male medical ward, walked through the vestibule, passed the main row of beds, and entered the tuberculosis ward.

Moses sat in the first bed cheerfully joking with his nearest neighbor. His walking stick leaned against the metal bedframe and his sandals were placed beside the bed where he could swing his legs down and stand up in the shoes. He turned to me immediately, his eyes lively and alert. I had not been on the ward in two weeks since I had been working with the pediatricians, and the change in Moses was dramatic. He was still having night sweats, he said, but his late afternoon fevers had finally died off. I saw that he breathed comfortably without oxygen.

"I am so grateful, doctor," he said.

"How long will you be here?" I said.

"Months," he said.

"Then what?"

Moses flashed a big grin. "Then home," he said.

We shook hands and I said I was happy to see him so much better. I told him I would be leaving Swaziland soon and that I would come to say goodbye before I left. He nodded and I went away from of the ward smiling.

Outside in the sunshine, I spotted Philomele hanging her colorful laundry in the mission yard. She waved me over and said that her stomach pains had resolved. The antibiotics were working and she was getting around well now, she said.

"Wonderful," I said.

"Thank you," she said. I did not want to interfere with a good thing so I asked no further questions and continued on past the newsstand and snack bar, and on to the clinic. In a moment, Nkosi dashed across my path, running alongside another child of about four. Nkosi was wearing a patterned shirt with nothing below the waist. I called his name. His friend kept running but he stopped in his tracks and looked cautiously in my direction. I went up to him and put a hand on his back. He looked up at me with his enormous round eyes and remained standing there with his arms at his side. I took the stethoscope out and listened to his lungs. I noted that his swollen stomach had receded. He had gained eleven pounds since coming to the hospital and the abscesses had melted back. There had been no fever in nearly two weeks. An aunt had materialized and lived by his bedside now, plying him with provisions when he returned from running through the mission with children he had befriended. I could see that he had emerged back into the world and was taking on the size and shape of a normal four-year-old. Mikibi's plan was to continue his accelerated nutrition for another week or two and then send him home with the aunt, who would care for him and take him sometimes to visit his brothers and sisters.

"Okay, Nkosi, goodbye," I said, patting him firmly on the back. He held my gaze for a moment, then disappeared in the direction of his playmate.

Near the end of my stay in Swaziland, Tsembayena chased me down in front of the emergency room and said breathlessly, "My father would like to talk with you about his diabetes. Can you talk to him when you come to the homestead on Sunday?"

I protested that her father would get much more professional advice through the Defense Department clinics and if he needed help he should visit his doctor immediately. Tsem shook her head firmly. Her sister Khetsiwe's rash had cleared up rapidly after using the antibiotics I'd sent her, and news of the cure had apparently spread. Tsem insisted her father wanted to meet with me, so I relented.

On Sunday afternoon Tsem's brother arrived at the mission and we piled into the back of the family pickup that he piloted. We drove past the dusty soccer field, where another match was under way, and turned onto the road to Mbabane. Tsem's brother drove ten kilometers along the highway and then turned sharply onto a bumpy dirt road. We stopped momentarily to pick up two hitchhikers and then continued toward a steep green mountain. As we came closer I saw a waterfall plunging down a steep ravine. We stopped for the hitchhikers to scramble off the bed of the truck, continued up the road for a few minutes, and then rolled to a stop in front of a cluster of mud-brick houses. Chickens squawked and scattered in the unsettled dust. Tsem explained that her father and two of his brothers along with their immediate families lived on the homestead. I unfolded myself from the cab and shook out the cramps in my legs. Off to one side was a garden of squash running in a long strip next to the huts.

"It is common for the men to take more than one wife," Tsem said. She'd told me before that her father had two other wives, neither of whom lived on the homestead.

Tsem led me to her parents' house, a concrete structure in the center of the compound. On the front porch, I shook hands with her smiling mother, who wore a bright red scarf over her head and traditional Swazi dress, a long cloth wrapped around her waist and another that covered one shoulder. She said Tsem's father would come outside in a few minutes and suggested we go walking. Tsem took my arm, and her youngest sister followed us along. We walked past three pigs snorting in the dust and came to a house under construction. The walls of the house had been framed with thick tree branches in a square and rocks had been stacked in place between the branches. Tsem explained that dusty soil would be mixed with water to make mud paste and then poured over the rocks and branches. The sun would bake the mud and the walls would harden. It would take about one week to finish the house if the family worked nonstop.

Tsem pointed into the field at the family's cattle herd. The sister said, "Does your family keep cows?"

My father worked for Boeing then and I said, "We don't have cows. We make airplanes." The sister looked at me like I was crazy.

We moved on and Tsem introduced me to a seamstress who ran a business out of her windowless concrete house making children's clothes. Inside were dirt floors and harsh yellow light from an uncovered light bulb. In a few moments we came outside again into the red-gold afternoon and circled to the top of the homestead, passing an enormous wooden pen filled with maize. Dried rows of kernels had shrunk down on the cobs. A chicken standing beside the pen pecked determinedly at the wood fence. Then we turned back to her parents' house. Now her father sat in a rocking chair on the porch. He wore navy-colored trousers and a western-style white collared shirt open at the neck. Tsem's mother leaned on the porch railing. Tsem gestured at a folding chair facing her father.

"Hello, doctor," he said, rising to shake my hand.

"Hello, Mr. Dlamini. It's nice to meet you." I slipped into the chair and watched him sit down carefully in the rocker. His hands were knotted with arthritis and he looked to be about sixty years old.

"Doctor, I have diabetes," he said in a grave tone of voice. "They say my kidneys might be affected. What can be done?"

I pushed myself back in the chair and crossed my legs.

"How long have you had diabetes?" I said.

"Three or four years," he said.

"Do you measure your blood sugars?" I said.

"No, doctor, but I have had some tests recently and they say the sugar is high."

His wife straightened up. "But," she said, and interjected in rapid Siswati.

"She says he doesn't eat any sugar at all," Tsem said.

"How are your eyes?"

"They are not so good, doctor. I cannot see well at night and the vision is blurry."

"Do you have pain or numbness in your feet?"

"I have no problems with my feet, doctor."

"Do you check your feet?"

"Excuse me, doctor?"

"You should check your feet every day for blisters or cuts," I said. "I'll show you in a moment." I glanced over at his wife and then at Tsem and she translated.

"Do you take medication?" I asked.

He gestured at his wife and she produced a bottle of pills. I turned the bottle around in my hand, read the label, twisted off the cap, and shook the round orange tablets that skittered across the bottom.

"How often do you take this?"

"Every so often, when my sugar is high."

"Any other medications?"

"Just this, doctor."

Tsem and her mother looked intently at me.

"And is your blood pressure normal or high?"

"It is high, doctor."

I reached for the stethoscope I had brought with me in a bag. Tsem and her mother sat up attentively now. A clutch of children had gathered and were watching the visit. Mr. Dlamini seemed to enjoy being the center of the spectacle, so I said nothing and began the examination. I looked in his eyes and mouth, felt carefully under his chin, listened to the steady rhythm of his heart. I crouched down, removed his shoes and socks, and instructed him how to check between the toes for early signs of infection. "Diabetics can get bad infections and it is best to catch them early." I straightened one of his legs and studied the sole of his foot, musing how I'd seen very few patients in Swaziland with long-term diseases like diabetes, and I realized that having such diseases depended on having survived malaria and tuberculosis and HIV.

Finally I stood up and said, "You will always have diabetes. There's no cure for diabetes, even in America."

The patient nodded gravely and his wife gasped. I glanced in her direction and said, "The goal is to bring your blood sugar back to normal to protect your eyes, nerves, and kidneys. You have to take your medicine every day. You want to make your blood sugar normal every day. You can't just take it when you feel sick. I want you to check your feet every day like I showed you. Also, I think you should be on medicine for blood pressure."

"The government can give me the medicine," he said. He rose from his chair and held his hand out to me.

"Thank you, doctor," he said.

"Thank you, doctor," his wife murmured.

I shook Mr. Dlamini's hand and nodded to his wife and put my stethoscope back in the bag. Tsem folded the chairs and the children had moved off in search of new adventure. The front porch cleared. The daylight had started to die.

Tsem smiled and touched my arm. "Thank you again," she said.

"I hope that helps," I said to Mr. Dlamini.

Tsem's mother smiled broadly at us and then made hand motions shooing us off the porch.

Tsem said, "Let's go have dinner now. We've killed a chicken in your honor."

Chapter 7

Dillon

A fter morning clinic I hustle out the back door with a knot in my stomach. I'm overdue for a conversation with seventy-year-old Edith Pierce, who was born and raised on a ranch outside Dillon, Montana. She was admitted to hospital bed No. 4 after turning a bold shade of yellow last week that stained her tongue and brightly tinted her silver hair. Edith is one of Dillon's social lights. She clerked at the Quality Feed all her adult life, trafficking in news and messages and chatter, and is known and loved all over town. Two years ago, she fell from a horse and she bled into her brain. She swallows nightly medicine now to prevent seizures, and her speech sounds like putty squeezed from a tube. She's hasn't been the same since the accident.

The yellow jaundice came on so disarmingly. Edith feels healthy, doesn't hurt, has no vomiting or diarrhea, no fevers or night sweats. She wonders if she's lost weight, and at a glance I'm fairly sure she has. The story flows easily and the diagnosis arrives in her telling, confirmed by ultrasound. A day later, a scope passed into her small intestine visualizes the footprint of a pancreatic tumor eroding through her bile ducts.

Now I cross the back lawn of the medical center, aimed toward the hospital. The gusting wind lifts my hair and makes my pant legs quiver and snap. The air is warm with sunshine and smells like fall. This morning a patient has brought news of snow at 6,200 feet, and I wonder when we'll have snow in town.

I turn through the staff entrance and walk briskly through the hall to Edith's room. From the door I see a television flashing on mute in a high corner. Edith lies in bed under the covers. Her face is bony with freckles over her cheeks and she stares indifferently at the ceiling. She wears a long, green velvet nightgown. The window by the bed is open despite the cool weather; since the accident Edith leaves a window open to keep from feeling she's choking. Her husband, Carl, stands by the far wall of the room, his hefty canvas ranch jacket buttoned all the way up, a black felt cowboy hat atop his head. I've never seen him without the hat.

"Hello again," Edith says, swinging her legs stiffly over the edge of the bed. I touch her shoulder and greet her.

"Good morning," I say, nodding to Carl. "Glad to see you."

"How are you, doctor?" Carl says. His voice is hoarse and dry, and he comes around the bed so he can hear me.

Edith and Carl know about her pancreatic cancer, about its regional spread, about her three months or so to live. They've faced the news bravely. Earlier in the week we discussed chemotherapy and she rightfully declined. What's at stake now is determining how she'll spend her remaining days. Carl has made his mission known: he intends to take her home.

I'm concerned that Carl can't manage all that she needs. She's considerably weaker from the weight loss and can hardly sit up without help, after lying in bed the past week. I've learned that she doesn't eat three meals a day at home, that delivered lunches are pushed six deep in the refrigerator because Carl doesn't set up the trays for her. The house is in complete disarray, and her family has pleaded that I not send her home until one of the children comes next month to clear out the place.

Still, I can't keep Edith in the hospital, since she doesn't have an acute problem requiring hour-to-hour nursing surveillance.

"We've got to talk about leaving the hospital," I say, shaking Carl's hand. I've already considered every possible way to present the idea that Edith ought to go to the nursing home, where care isn't the same quality since a health care chain bought the facility six years ago.

"You'd like to get home and Carl wants to bring you home, and we need a plan for getting you there."

"Yes," Carl says firmly.

I take a breath in and say, "Edith, you're not strong enough to be at home right now. You've got to be able to get out of bed and to the bathroom and around the house. Today, the therapists say you're not strong enough yet."

"I know," she says. "I can feel it."

"But I'll take care of her," Carl says.

"I've taken care of a hundred cancer patients," I say. "What I learned is that you can't do everything for her. That's a trap. You'll get so tired that you can't enjoy being with her. That's why we have home nurses and caregivers and therapists. That's why we have places like nursing homes." I nod my head at the words "nursing home."

Carl quickly says, "Oh, no."

I level my gaze with Carl's. "Edith's got to be strong enough to get up and around, and right now, she's not. If she's sitting in bed all day, she'll keep getting weaker, and that could kill her. If she's sitting in bed all day, she's also at high risk for a blood clot, and that could kill her."

Carl freezes like he does every time Edith's imminent dying comes up. He understands the seriousness of her illness, and that's why he is so desperate to take her home. He can't bear for her to die in a nursing home.

"A nursing home doesn't mean you gave up on her. It doesn't mean you can't see her. You can be with her from morning until night. You can walk with her and help her build strength. You can actually enjoy your time with her."

Carl's eyes have turned red and watery and Edith stares blankly into the hallway.

"This is what I suggest," I say. "You go to the nursing home for ten days and let the physical therapist give you a good workout and get your muscles back. You'll get hot meals and gain some weight, or at least not lose any more. Then we'll know you can go home safely."

I'm being presumptuous, having known them all of four days, never having visited their home or met their extended family, and yet I've already decided what's best for her. But doctoring calls for this kind of judgment, and I believe the plan will give her more time at home in the end. It would be cynical to send her home just to teach them that she'll fail, and charge Edith the price of further weakening. I've seen that happen, and I'd be misleading them to suggest otherwise. I just can't see another way to negotiate the issue.

Carl and I regard each other silently. I know he's not

convinced this plan will help Edith at all. Then, Edith speaks.

"I think we should do that. That's a good plan," she says. Edith has told relatives that she doesn't think she can make it at home. Carl's jaw slackens. The one thing we agree on is that we have to honor Edith's wishes.

"What I don't like is the way they put her to bed and forget about her there," he says.

"I'll make sure they get her up," I say. "She can't stay in bed all day. She's got to be up for a few hours every day, at least."

"That's a good idea," Edith says.

Nine years have elapsed since I first touched down on the tundra, donned a stethoscope, and began hearing stories of disease and recovery from people who inhabit some of the most remote parts of the Pacific Northwest. Soon I was absorbed into the contours of rural people and places, and privy to a kind of doctoring unknown in the big academic hospitals.

On the heels of the WWAMI experience, I chose a general internal medicine residency with a rural year in Idaho, intending to gain broad skills to practice in a remote setting. The Idaho year brought much of the same magic, fashioning a rural community for me from the 150 war veterans I followed in clinic, through emergency room and hospital visits, and back to their homes and lives. For the third and last year of residency I returned to Seattle, rubbed elbows with academic subspecialists, and batted about the possibility of fellowship training, perhaps in infectious disease, perhaps in pulmonary medicine, which would anchor me to an academic research center or private practice in a city. I admired many of my teaching physicians as brilliant scientists and intellectuals, and for a time fancied myself in that vein. But WWAMI had imprinted on me that doctors take care of patients, and in the end I could not imagine a lifetime of doctoring without patients at the center.

Residency ended and I was suddenly an attending physician, a full-blooded general internist. Practices in Bozeman and Livingston, Montana, and Soldotna, Alaska, were actively recruiting and I considered the positions briefly. After much thought I realized that Seattle was still home, that I wasn't ready to make the leap to the open country. I signed on to take care of inpatients from a refugee and homeless population at the Seattle county hospital. The community stretches down Yesler Way hill into parks on First and Third Avenues, takes in the waterfront and the Chief Sealth Club, where the homeless shower and do laundry, and the downtown Emergency Service Center. It's thoroughly urban, but like any remote town, has a defined community of people and distinct sense of place.

A colleague coaxed me back to WWAMI-land with images of the wide, green Big Hole Valley, aspens along the Madison River, and sleek Montana trout, images that trickled through my inbox over two years. He'd worked in Dillon during residency and effused over the quality of doctors and patients. Dillon is a ranch town an hour's drive from the nearest specialist, with a small liberal arts college and mountains everywhere. He was certain I'd like the place, and it took minimum convincing to have me cover two vacationing internists for a month.

I arranged a hiatus from the Seattle job and some months later drove the 650 miles out to southwest Montana. When I eased off the highway into town, I remembered having filled my gas tank in Dillon once, on the long haul between Spokane, where the world was pregnant women, and Pocatello, where the world became sick children. The same orange light was falling on the mountains down the wide valley going south into Idaho, and my memory was crisp with how eager I'd been to get to Pocatello. I had high hopes for the kind of doctor that place would make of me.

As I drove through downtown Dillon at dusk, the old familiar excitement returned. WWAMI had given me intense glimpses into the human experience, and I believed a WWAMI rotation would still have relevant lessons for a practicing doctor. All about me now was the promise of a new story and a fresh take on medical practice.

Dillon is farther removed from civilization than most people can stand. The small clinic and fifteen-bed hospital serve twelve thousand people in a high desert valley that, at 5,542 square miles, is considerably larger than the state of Connecticut. Montana Street, the main strip, offers one good Mexican restaurant, storage and loading docks for the Williams Feed Company, Johnson's saddlery, several fly fishing services, an Elks lodge, several bars, a hardware store, and chain grocer. The sun shines relentlessly and there are soft mountains just beyond town that seem made from the velvet of deer antlers. The town sits at 5,000 feet elevation, and the dry air crackles.

In just a few weeks, I've begun to know the place. A patient this morning describes his plans for elk season and his recent years' luck at drawing hunting tags; he goes as far as saying he hunts down near the Idaho border. A young wife cries to me in the hospital waiting room, heartbroken over a cheating older husband, undecided if she will sell the family cows and divorce him. A cattle auctioneer wonders about mystery chest pains that peak in the busy season, and a rancher postpones his return visit until haying is finished. Last weekend I took in the skillful calf roping and bronco riding at the fairgrounds just beyond my neighborhood, and it's posted that Anderson Ranch will auction cattle at the south end of the parking lot this weekend. From patients I learn that beef prices are up 33 percent this season and rising, and the news cheers locals. In the afternoon, an elderly man who helps on his brother's ranch will come in with an angry-looking leg, three days after a cow kicked him, and he will say, "The leg itself feels fine, but I just can't stand."

Now I remember what it feels like to take care of patients over a lifetime. Rural patients bring concerns to the clinic and trust the doctor to take care of them, without handing them off to a second or third person. The rural doctor sees patients who may barter for medical advice with several dozen eggs, a truckload of firewood, or plumbing repairs. Doctor and patient cross paths at the grocery store, in the bleachers at the high school football game, on a neighborhood sidewalk. Now I remember: this is a relationship that extends into most places where people live their days, and privileges the doctor with a view of the patient as a human being.

Carl drops by the clinic later in the afternoon and says he doesn't understand. He thought he and Edith were going home but now Edith is slated for the nursing home, which he believes will do irreparable harm. I pick up the message on my way out of town for the weekend, and in a moment I'm heading back to the hospital. Edith is taking a turn around the ward on Carl's arm, and they follow me into her cold room. Edith takes short, uneven steps, bends at the waist, and before I know what's happening, falls to sitting on the bed.

Edith takes several heavy breaths and says, "I think I ought to go home."

"I think we had a misunderstanding," I say, holding her arm to help her balance.

"We can't leave her in that nursing home," Carl says. "They'll put her to bed and make her stay there, pay no attention to her."

I stand at the foot of Edith's bed. Edith is thin and jaundiced, and her eyes and cheeks pop so prominently from her face that she seems hollow.

"Maybe we can make a deal."

Carl waits with his hands in his jacket pockets.

"You go to the nursing home for the weekend and give therapy a try. I'll visit on Monday or Tuesday and see how you're doing. If it goes badly and you're not getting stronger, Carl can take you home immediately. We'll set up the home nursing and meals we talked about. That way you can try out the rehab and have a way out if there are problems. Do you think that would work?"

Edith says, "I think that's a fine idea."

Facing Edith, I say, "We are not going to leave you there. I promise that. But you have to promise me to give rehab a fair try."

"That's just fine, honey," Edith says.

"I'd like everyone to feel we're working on this together," I say.

"Okay, we can agree on that," Carl says, fumbling in his pockets. "We'll talk Monday. I have my cell phone with me all the time. You can call it." He brings out the slim, silver phone that folds out to talk and Edith's sister copies the number down on a slip of paper.

"I'll wait for your call," Carl says.

I saw from the very beginning that a doctor should understand how people live, a truth that is as relevant for me now as for any practicing orthopedic surgeon or oncologist. The problem is imparting that wisdom to a book-smart twenty-three-year-old medical student who hails from the sheltered suburbs. It would be disingenuous to think the human experience could be broken down and packaged into a course syllabus and eighteen lectures, as though it were cell physiology or the cardiovascular system, that a multiple-choice test could evaluate whether a student can competently interpret human feeling and desire.

The first lesson of medicine is that almost everything important comes from the patient's story. That story occupies center stage in the rural setting and became my vehicle to tap into a the human experience. Patients talk to me about families and homes and how they hope to live, and they allow me into acts and events with deeply human consequences, like a thwarted pregnancy or prolonged life support or attempted suicide. In years of training and practice, I've been close to innumerable human mileposts, and that proximal knowledge gives me credibility when advising a seventy-year-old on how to live and die.

The patient narrative allows more than access to the human heart. The narrative gives the most relevant information on a patient's condition and provides a starting point for the plan. In medical school I conducted lengthy patient interviews and wrote epic chart notes that chased down every thread of health and disease, arriving after lengthy discussion at a most likely diagnosis. In a thousand renderings of the patient's story, I gradually understood the elements a story turns on. Sometime during my last year of residency, seven years along, patients' reports of symptoms and sensations and fragments of events began to fall together into stories I recognized. Now I know to keep at a conversation with the patient until a picture materializes. I know from stories experienced doctors tell that my sense of the patient's narrative will continue to evolve and deepen.

The patient story is the most human element in medical practice, and inherently the most dangerous. In internal medicine, the story is often about a body's slow decline, about its demons, and arrives eventually and sometimes suddenly to the prospect of loss and death. That story has provided me much grief over the years and made me cold and empty amidst the most extreme suffering. I don't believe a story grips or horrifies or saddens me in quite the same way it did at first pass in

WWAMI-land, or in Africa; I'm just not as good a doctor when I'm preoccupied with one person's saga. But sometimes the story is the highest reward of doctoring, a window into human will and perseverance. Sometimes I enter a story and find I can bring a little light and relief to human suffering.

For now, when I face Edith in the morning, my disbelief and sadness and hope for small gains moves just under the surface while we chat about her knobby fingers, her favorite quilt.

On Monday I return from hiking in fresh snowfall and the weekend doctor tells me that Edith and Carl have moved over to the nursing home without incident. I expected more last-minute resistance, so I'm surprised. In the morning it's so busy between clinic, the hospital, and emergency room that I postpone calling Carl until lunchtime and then until after clinic, and suddenly it's evening and too late. My nurse clucks sympathetically and blocks out later Tuesday afternoon so I can make nursing home rounds. She knows how much of a challenge it was getting Edith there and she wants me to make good on my promises. I'm curious for what I'll find on rounds. It's a good sign that we haven't heard from Carl.

After work on Tuesday, the resident and I drive to the edge of town. The nursing home is a one-story stucco compound with spindly starter trees along the front walk. Inside, the home is brightly lit and faintly steamy. Edith's room is on the back hallway. We pass an afternoon piano sing-along in the common room, where the voices are young and cheerful.

When we come in, Edith sits up pertly, crosses her legs, and smiles. She's considerably less jaundiced now after her bile duct was opened with wire mesh tubing and bile has started draining from her skin and nails. Carl is nowhere to be seen, and I remember my nurse mentioning that Carl has waited all day for his cows to come in. I should have known from sartorial clues that Carl ranches, but I'd assumed he was too old for such hard physical work. I'm pleased that he's shown me otherwise.

Edith shares the room with an elderly woman I've taken care of several times, and the husband at her side has also visited me in the clinic. I wave hello to both of them and politely draw the curtain.

"How are you, Edith?"

"My stomach hurts," she says, and suddenly lies back down.

"Did you get sick?"

"Feel like I want to be. If I move around I feel better."

Carl looms in the doorway wearing his black cowboy hat and talking on the cell phone. He sees me and says, "Got to go. Doctor's here." He snaps the silver phone closed and offers his broad hand.

"Your cows come in?"

He shakes his head, seems nonplussed. It's almost five o'clock and the sky is darkening.

"Edith's stomach is bothering her today," I say.

Carl says quickly, "But she was doing real good. She likes the therapy and they're working hard with her." He's so relaxed.

I move toward the bed to examine her stomach. She's wearing the same green velvet nightgown with lace trim across the chest, and I lift this off her legs so her stomach is exposed. There's no pain when I push down deeply over the colon or feel under her ribs for the liver and gallbladder. Then I step back, and Edith pops right up to a sitting position.

"I want to walk," she says, and stands slowly and steadily. Carl moves nimbly to her side and she clasps his arm.

"I'll have the nurses bring something for your stomach," I say.

Edith nods. "I'd appreciate if you could fix my stomach."

"What do you think?" I say to Carl.

"It's a little setback," he says. "If you can get her back on track, that would help."

"Another week or ten days here?"

"I think that would be fine," he says.

"I think that's a good idea," she says.

"Will you be ready at home?" I say.

After a moment, Carl says, "Yes."

I watch them turn down the long hall. Carl leads and Edith follows with steady fluid steps. They move with an enviable rhythm, like practiced dance partners. Edith's green velvet gown sways at her ankles. For a moment I believe I can see the future: Edith will grow stronger and go home to the farm in time for the early winter. Her sons and daughters, who've started to arrive, will postpone faraway lives to stay through Thanksgiving and Christmas, filling the house with light and sound. Edith and Carl will move together where her fate leads, with her doctor close by.

I'm in a place again where doctoring is a human act. I ache, watching Edith pass her last days, and I try to appreciate the grief that Carl is experiencing. I've learned that just being there helps moderate the sadness. It helps to visit the nursing home. It helps to run across Carl at the checkout line in the grocery store. And it will help, when Edith finally goes home, to call at the farm and peruse pictures of grandchildren and stand in the cold air hearing about the family steers. Everything helps.

Edith and Carl swing past the nurse's station now and Edith stops to catch her breath. I know and she knows and Carl knows that she's just walked two hundred yards, and that's as far as she has gone anytime in recent memory. Edith's skin faintly glows: It is no small miracle to be dying and yet becoming healed. Carl leans over and firmly grasps my arm. We regard each other for a long moment, Carl's gaze flinty and hopeful. Then he thanks me hoarsely, his eyes clear and dry, and they push off again.

Postscript

I teach at the medical school now. Every Friday morning, lecture hall is shuttered for an hour and I sit at a table with seven first-year medical students, reviewing their visits to the hospital wards. We talk about putting patients at ease during interviews. We discuss answering queries about where a student is from and whether she's married. We practice skills like eliciting how much alcohol a patient drinks and playact different ways of asking about HIV risk factors.

We watch the videotape of a medical student's interview with an elderly Texan woman who has a sarcoma. The student begins the conversation with several long-winded questions and suffers a loss of words when the patient appears to fall asleep.

In class I hint at the subtleties of interacting with sick people. I describe how I like to obtain a patient's story.

Mostly I get out of the way so the students can talk about what they see and hear on the wards. I sit back listening while they teach each other what they learn from patients.

A Brief History of WWAMI

<img style omitted decorative divider>

On orders from his boss, Jack Lein fired up his silver Mercury station wagon in 1965 and drove through towns across rural Washington state. Lein had recently joined the faculty of the University of Washington School of Medicine in Seattle and was charged with updating rural physicians on the latest medical practices. Lein discovered surprising facts about medicine outside of big cities. A solo Colville physician was struggling to find a second general practitioner to join him. The four-doctor practice in Tonasket had dwindled to one doctor of retirement age, and Forks was down to its last doctor, too. Statistics confirmed the drastic situation in the region. There were no doctors at all in 404 of 434 Alaska towns or across seven Montana counties. Patients traveled great distances for health care, and those who didn't travel received no health care at all.

In the preceding decade, 646 physicians had graduated from the University of Washington, and exactly one was practicing general medicine in rural Washington. A handful were GPs elsewhere; an incredible 608 graduates had gone into medical specialties.

The rural doctor was disappearing from the Pacific Northwest.

By the late 1960s, a GP named Ted Phillips had finally hit upon his ideal practice in Sitka, Alaska. He hailed from rural Ohio, the son of a general surgeon, and at the dinner table his father often spoke admiringly of the local GPs. Phillips had graduated at the top of his medical school class at Johns Hopkins, where the faculty and administration had cajoled and threatened him away from his dream of general practice, a pursuit that top students of the day never wasted talents on. But Phillips had prevailed in the end, heading successively farther westward with internship and then residency, and finally landing a Public Health Service job in Sitka. He loved the breadth of general practice. His patients needed pacemakers, so he learned to implant these. His patients had heart attacks, and he was determined to offer the most modern treatments.

When his government work obligation expired, he hung out his own shingle and began searching for a practice partner. He searched fruitlessly and then desperately and eventually understood that rural practice had reached a crisis point.

In 1969 the University of Washington hired Phillips to start up a new division of family medicine. He brought with him a bold idea for training future family physicians: "It was absolutely essential for students to go out where medicine was being practiced," he said.

Within a year of his arrival, the number of preclinical medical students planning on family practice careers jumped dramatically, numbering almost half of the class.

At a class meeting, a professor asked a first-year student why he was contemplating family medicine so eagerly. The student pointed to Phillips and said, "Because he's the real thing."

Jack Lein and colleagues at the University of Washington were also becoming vocal about the lack of doctors in small towns across the state. The social activism of the 1960s buzzed in school corridors, and progressive faculty members began agitating for serious change in physician education. A new concept emerged at a gathering of several faculty members and a GP from Omak, Washington, at a medical society meeting in September 1969. The new dean of the UW medical school, Robert Van Citters, poured the liquor and steered the conversation. Teaching general medicine at the university was thought impractical given the research and specialty bent in Seattle. Eventually Pres Bratrude, the GP, said, "Send me the residents and I'll teach them."

Associate Dean Gus Swanson wrote the proposal for an expanded medical school spanning the states of Washington, Alaska, Montana, and Idaho (WAMI), where students would take basic science classes in their home states and apprentice with rural physicians. The idea was that hometown exposure would encourage students to return to small communities and practice as generalists. Shortly afterward, Swanson pitched the proposal to the Commonwealth Fund, a health care foundation established by a New York heiress.

In December 1970 the Commonwealth Fund pledged $1 million in seed money, and WAMI was under way. Great excitement spread through the medical school. WAMI was the most significant change in physician education since 1910. For the wider faculty community, the concept of training medical students away from the university was either revolutionary or heresy.

University President Charles Odegaard gave full support to the risky experiment and predicted the coming faculty grumbling. "Don't ask the faculty to vote on it," he said. "Just go do it."

The first semester of medical education away from the university began under a magnifying lens in Fairbanks, Alaska, fifteen hundred miles from Seattle. The university rounded up nine first-year medical students from Washington and Alaska who liked the idea of bucking the establishment. A geneticist named Dick Lyons, who had roamed interior Alaska cataloguing chromosome disorders, was hired to teach the entire semester of basic sciences. Lyons latched onto the WAMI mission quickly. He sent each of his students to clinic with a local physician once every week. Later he hit on the idea of placing students in the Alaska bush alongside venturesome native Alaskan health aides. The students returned with tales of how primitive the practice of medicine was in the villages.

All that mattered to the deans in Seattle, though, was how the Alaska students performed on exams. Doubters would pounce on poor scores as evidence that medical students couldn't be trained away from the university. The students felt the growing pressure as the term wore on, and Lyons found himself providing mental health support in addition to teaching. He asked students if they were too cold that winter, how families were holding up, what they saw beyond graduation, and he helped several weather near-breakdowns.

Roy Schwarz, the first director for WAMI affairs, flew to Fairbanks after the semester ended bearing the news that the Alaska students had performed on par with the Seattle students —except in anatomy, where they scored highest in the class thanks to Lyons's revival of cadaver dissection. The small classroom filled with relief and excitement. Lyons said, "What we learned was that we ought to do it again."

Medical students from Seattle began venturing eagerly to Omak, Washington, and to Kodiak, Alaska, to try clinical medicine in small places. The program unfolded as hoped. Video footage from 1972 shows a floatplane landing at dusk in a picturesque harbor and third-year medical student Jim McHugh alighting onto the dock at Spruce Island, an Alaska village of about three hundred natives. A middle-aged native woman approaches the thickly bearded McHugh to ask about her diabetes before he is even off the dock. The camera cuts to a clinic where he is peering into a child's ears and saying, "I never saw an ear infection or inflamed tonsils at the University of Washington; now I am seeing five to ten a day."

More than thirty years later McHugh remembers the immaculate graveyards overflowing with small crosses marking each infant death, and beautiful Orthodox churches that played a prominent role in the community of devout villagers. At the end of the video, McHugh sits with an interviewer and says the rotation will help him decide if he'll become a small-town doctor. He says his wife will visit him in Kodiak and they'll decide together if they can live in a place that small.

McHugh signs off and then another counterculture type comes on screen and says, "Seattle's just a place to plug in and do your time."

As far as the students were concerned, the real action was in WAMI-land.

For the ambitious young deans in Seattle, however, the heat was on. WAMI had stirred up great controversy in the academic world. The president of the American Association of Medical Colleges, Sherman Melinkoff, had roundly chastised the Seattle crew at a national meeting. "The University of Washington is ruining medical education as we know it," he said. He harangued the group about the inferior education medical students received in Fairbanks, far from the academic center.

There was pressure at home, too. WAMI was running out of seed money and the university needed to convince state legislatures to begin funding their state's medical students. Jack Lein, the savvy and politically connected head of postgraduate education, became the WAMI pitchman. Lein met with legislators in each of the four states, flashing homemade slides about the rural health crisis, lobbying the governors relentlessly, and playing a film reel full of WAMI testimony that a producer at the Disney Company had patched together. He put Ted Phillips on stage as often as possible.

"There was the general feeling that the country was losing Marcus Welby, MD," Lein said.

At Lein's urging, U.S. Senator Warren Magnuson of Washington added $7 million to the Health Manpower Act of 1972 to keep WAMI alive.

In 1973 a family practice resident named Roger Rosenblatt volunteered to scout out a proposed WAMI rotation in Grandview, Washington, a damp agricultural town with a large seasonal farmworker population. He had arrived in Seattle with stellar recommendations from Harvard Medical School, where he'd also been so involved in the antiwar movement that he generated an arrest record. He picked Seattle because WAMI fit with his idea of socially responsible medicine. As a resident physician, he continued to dress in the 1960s fashion. At the medical society meeting in conservative Grandview, his unruly beard and ponytailed hair drew hisses and boos from local physicians.

Regardless, Rosenblatt was smitten with rural medicine. He greatly admired the depth of practice that the attending GPs handled and was overjoyed to finally learn practical medical skills. He was also dismayed by the limited care that could be delivered in that small town and the primitive conditions of the nearest hospital, ten miles away.

In his last year of residency, he spent two months in Omak with the GP, Pres Bratrude. He loved WAMI-land so much that he began building a cabin on 140 acres of second-growth forest near Omak, and he worked on the house while taking hospital calls on a two-way radio. One snowy afternoon he walked a salvaged window frame a mile and a half into the cabin. He raised the roof that summer with fellow residents and faculty in the department of family medicine.

After Rosenblatt's residency, Senator Magnuson tapped him to develop new physician offices in the rural Northwest and placed at his disposal millions of dollars for salaries and new outpatient offices. Rosenblatt recruited tirelessly, luring colleagues dedicated to social activism to rural Washington.

In two years he helped to establish new practices in twenty-five towns that had no physician. Most of the practices are still healthy and successful today.

Three years into the WAMI program, medical school faculty reached the consensus that WAMI education was as high quality as that at Seattle's teaching hospitals.

Five years in, the university faculty voted to continue WAMI, and the four state legislatures began funding the training program.

Seven years in, the UW and WAMI program received full accreditation from the American Association of Medical Colleges.

Ten years in, Roger Rosenblatt showed that WAMI students chose primary care careers and rural practice at double the rate of medical students anywhere else.

In 1997, Wyoming joined the regional consortium, and WAMI became WWAMI. As of 2004, seventy-six UW medical students spend their first year in their home states; they join the one hundred Seattle students in second year. Students can elect third- and fourth-year clinical rotations in every core medical field at more than one hundred sites in small and midsized towns in the five WWAMI states.

More than 90 percent of UW students experience one or more WWAMI placements, half opted for a primary care residency, and one-quarter practice in a rural setting. The University of Washington has been ranked the No. 1 primary care medical school by US News and World Report for the past ten years, and WWAMI has been the centerpiece of its strong reputation.

Roger Rosenblatt's cabin on the Okanogan still stands, providing year-round shelter for medical students and residents rotating with the family physicians of Omak.